EMBRACING THE TRANSFORMATION

Embracing the Transformation

WALTER BRUEGGEMANN

Edited by K. C. Hanson

CASCADE *Books* • Eugene, Oregon

EMBRACING THE TRANSFORMATION

Cascade Books
An Imprint of Wipf and Stock Publishers
199 W. 8th Ave., Suite 3
Eugene, OR 97401

www.wipfandstock.com

ISBN 13: 978-1-62032-264-2

Cataloging-in-Publication data:

Brueggemann, Walter.

    Embracing the transformation / Walter Brueggemann ; edited by K. C. Hanson.

    x + 104 p.; 21.5 cm. Includes bibliographical references and indexes.

    ISBN 13: 978-1-62032-264-2

    1. Preaching. 2. Bible. O.T.—Homiletical use. I. Hanson, K. C. (Kenneth C.). II. Title.

BS1191.5 B75 2014

Manufactured in the USA

Contents

Foreword

IN READING WALTER BRUEGGEMANN'S writings on preaching from Old Testament texts I am always struck by his attention to point of view, community, and seeking justice.

In terms of point of view, he scrutinizes the unique vantage point of texts in terms of their stance toward the community being addressed, Yahweh's relationship to that community, and the self-awareness of the text's voice. The focus on traditions is also at work here: How are the traditions related to creation, the patriarchs/matriarchs, exodus, kingship, and Zion incorporated, challenged, reworked, or seen from a different angle?

Examining community, he repeatedly highlights the boundaries of and the ties that bind that community, the people and forces that work against that community for power and self-interest, and the desire for healthy and nurturing community that issues from the divine call. But also at stake here—in the ancient texts and in the Church—is challenging the status quo, investigating how community can be shaped despite the pressures of empire and the temptations of power.

And justice-seeking is given prominent place in Brueggemann's work. How are those on the margin treated? How do the economic interests of the elites vs. the peasants and the destitute come into play? How does the prophetic voice call into question the ethos of those with power?

While we do not live in the same world as ancient Israel and Judah, Brueggemann effectively shines a light on how questions of fidelity, community, and power that are raised in these ancient texts also impinge on our own identity, both individually and corporately. He is a faithful guide on this journey.

Preface

I AM DELIGHTED THAT these essays from the *Journal of Preachers* can be reissued in a more accessible form. I am grateful to Erskine Clarke, editor of the *Journal*, for his permission and encouragement for the republication. I am grateful to K. C. Hanson and his colleagues at Wipf and Stock for doing the heavy lifting of republication.

My review of these several pieces evokes two responses for me. On the one hand, I am aware that some of the bibliography is now a bit dated. But that is what we were reading and what seemed important at the time. On the other hand, I am somewhat surprised about the ways my own thinking has been clarified and sharpened since I wrote these pieces.

The accent on imagination seems to me of critical importance now. Such probing imagination is not simply playful artistry. It is rather the capacity to think and notice outside the frame of reference of dominant ideology. That frame of reference concerns the all-embracing market ideology that is attached, in our circumstance, to a broad and deep sense of U.S. exceptionalism. The combination of market ideology (that reduces everything to commodity and therefore to endless production and acquisition) and U.S. exceptionalism (that bespeaks privilege and entitlement) attests to a wondrous life of well-being. Except that it cannot be sustained. Except that it comes at immense cost to those who are left out of the market and who are not "qualified" for that exception. The intent of that combination is totalization. It intends to account for everything and intends to allow for nothing outside of that frame of reference.

It is easy enough to suggest that the orgy of the Superbowl, with its fantasy of money, power, sexuality, and self-indulgence is the central liturgy of that dominant ideology has been made into the national festival of self-congratulations. That liturgy (together with the ideology to which it attests) is an act of huge imagination. It imagines that the game matters. It imagines that the ads are significant. It imagines that betting on the game and everything connected to it is legitimate. It imagines that being in the environment of the game is important, even if the ticket prices preclude admission.

And then along comes the preaching task with its hard strategic decisions, either to ally with that liturgy and find there some possible outcomes of generosity and compassion . . . or to take the dire step outside that claim in order to imagine a society shaped by neighborly justice, economic righteousness, and covenantal faithfulness. It is not clear at all that such imagination outside dominant ideology is at all possible, any more than Mosaic imagination could succeed outside of Pharaoh's domain or that Jesus could make it outside of the hegemony of Rome. Of course the preacher is readily surrounded by vigilant advocates of market hegemony. And of course the preacher herself is inured in that ideology and its gamesmanship.

I hope that these articles may be something of a practical resource and reassurance for my fellow preachers who may be tempted, in hard circumstance, to stay on the surface of possible good gestures that are themselves not unimportant. The harder and urgent task is to go beneath such possible gestures to the deep claims of power, truth, and possibility where our future is at stake. Our social context for preaching is clearer than it has been in recent time. That, of course, does not make it any easier!

Walter Brueggemann
Epiphany 2013

1

An Imaginative "Or"

PERHAPS THE ASSIGNED THEME, "Preaching from the Old Testament," is intended to raise the sticky christological issue about finishing up Old Testament texts with Jesus.[1] The question is difficult and I should say where I am. I believe the Old Testament leads to the New and to the gospel of Jesus Christ. It does not, however, lead there directly, but only with immense interpretive agility. It does not, moreover, lead there singularly and necessarily in my judgment, because it also leads to Judaism and to the synagogue with its parallel faith. I shall bracket out of my consideration the christological question with the recognition, put in trinitarian terms, that in the Old Testament we speak of the Father of the Son.[2] As we confess the fullness of the Father manifest in the Son, so we may confess the fullness of God manifest to Israel in the Father. This is a question of endless dispute, but I owe it to you to be clear on my own conviction.

---

1. This is a slightly abbreviated version of my address to the annual meeting of The Academy of Homiletics in Toronto on December 3, 1998.

2. Levenson, *The Death and Resurrection of the Beloved Son*, has explored Jewish antecedents to the Christian foundation of "Father–Son."

An Alternative Community

Rather than the christological question, I shall focus on the ecclesial question. I understand preaching to be the chance to *summon and nurture an alternative community with an alternative identity, vision, and vocation, preoccupied with praise and obedience toward the God we Christians know fully in Jesus of Nazareth.* (This accent on alternative community resonates with the point being made in current "Gospel and Culture" conversations, much propelled by Lesslie Newbigin's focus on election, that God in God's inscrutable wisdom has chosen a people whereby the creation will be brought to wholeness.)[3] Two other beginning points make the community-forming work of the Old Testament peculiarly contemporary for us.

First, it is crucial to remember that the Old Testament is zealously and pervasively a Jewish book. Jews, and Israelites before them, are characteristically presented and understand themselves to be a distinct community with an alternative identity *rooted theologically and exhibited ethically*—alternative to the Egyptians, the Canaanites, the Philistines, the Assyrians, the Babylonians, the Persians, and the Hellenists—not only alternative, but always subordinate to and under threat from a dominant culture.[4] Thus I understand the intention of the Torah and Prophets—and differently I believe also Wisdom—to be insisting upon *difference* with theological rootage and ethical exhibit. The God-question is decisive, even if backgrounded; but the urgency concerns maintenance of communal identity, consciousness, and intentionality.

Second, with the disestablishment of Western Christianity and the collapse of the social hegemony of the church, the formation of a distinctive community of praise and obedience now becomes urgent as it had not been when the Western church could count on the support and collusion of the dominant culture.[5] If the church

---

3. For a critical summary of Newbigin's accent on ecclesiology, see Hunsberger, *Bearing the Witness of the Spirit.*

4. See Brueggemann, "Ecumenism as the Shared Practice of a Peculiar Identity."

5. See the most recent works by Douglas John Hall: *Waiting for Gospel*; and *What Christianity Is Not.*

in our society is not to evaporate into an ocean of consumerism and anti-neighborly individualism, then the summons and nurture of an alternative community constitutes an emergency. Thus with a huge *mutatis mutandis*, I propose that as the Jews lived in a perennial emergency of identity, so the church in our time and place lives in such an emergency.[6] In both cases, moreover, a primal response to the emergency and a primal antidote to assimilation and evaporation is the chance of preaching. In reflection upon the Old Testament and the ecclesial emergency, I will consider three theses.

The Clear Articulation of Either/Or

The summons and nurture, formation and enhancement of an alternative community of praise and obedience *depends upon the clear articulation of an either/or, the offer of a choice and the requirement of a decision that is theologically rooted and ethically exhibited, that touches and pervades every facet of the life of the community and its members.*[7] The choice is presented as clear. I believe that this *either/or* belongs inevitably to an alternative community, because an alternative identity requires an endless intentionality. For without

6. See my discussion in Brueggemann, *Cadences of Home.*

7. The *either/or* I will exposit is essentially that of the Deuteronomic theology that speaks with conviction that one choice is good and one is bad (see Deut 30:15–20). That is to say that the *either/or* of the Deuteronomist is completely without the irony of which Søren Kierkegaard can write (*Either/Or I*, 38–39):

Marry, and you will regret it. Do not marry, and you will also regret it. Marry or do not marry, you will regret it either way. Whether you marry or you do not marry, you will regret it either way. Laugh at the stupidities of the world, and you will regret it; weep over them, and you will also regret it. Laugh at the stupidities of the world or weep over them, you will regret it either way. Whether you laugh at the stupidities of the world or you weep over them, you will regret it either way. Trust a girl, and you will regret it. Do not trust her, and you will also regret it. Trust a girl or do not trust her, you will regret it either way. Whether you trust a girl or do not trust her, you will regret it either way. Hang yourself, and you will regret it. Do not hang yourself, and you will also regret it. Hang yourself or do not hang yourself, you will regret it either way. Whether you hang yourself or do not hang yourself, you will regret it either way. This, gentlemen, is the quintessence of all the wisdom of life.

vigilance the alternative cannot be sustained. I have reflected upon Old Testament texts around this theme; my impression is that there are only rare texts that are "holding actions." Everything in Israel's text urges an alternative.

The alternative that must be embraced in order to be Israel includes the summons to Abraham and Sarah to "go," for without going there will be no land and no future, no heir and no Israel. The summons to slaves in Egypt through Moses is to "depart," for if there is no "departure" there is no promised land. Moses worries, moreover, that if Israel does not believe, it will not depart and will not be Israel (Exod 4:1).[8] Less instantaneous but certainly pervasively, the prophets endlessly summon Israel to an alternative covenant ethic, lest the community be destroyed. And even in the wisdom traditions, the restrained advocacy of wisdom and righteousness is in the awareness that foolishness will indeed bring termination. Perhaps the most dominant statement of *either/or* that belongs characteristically to the faith perspective of the Old Testament is the context at Mt. Carmel where Elijah challenges Israel: "How long will you go limping with two different opinions? If Yahweh is God, follow him; but if Baal, then follow him" (1 Kgs 18:21a). We are told first, "The people did not answer him a word" (v. 21b). But at the end they said, "Yahweh indeed is God; Yahweh indeed is God" (v. 39). This text knows that Israel, in order to be the people of Yahweh, must be endlessly engaged in an intentional decision for Yahwism, a decision that fends off the powerful forces of the dominant culture.[9]

Joshua 24

I wish now to consider in some detail two classic formulations of *either/or* that occur at pivotal points in Israel's life. The first of these is Joshua 24, a much discussed text that von Rad regarded as an

---

8. It is instructive that in both narratives of Abraham (Gen 15:6) and Moses (Exod 4:1), the key term is *'men* = "trust." It is "trust" that makes the "or" of Yahweh choosable against the "either" that characteristically seems given and easy to embrace.

9. Of that intentional decision, Neusner writes, "All of us are Jews through the power of our imagination." *The Enchantments of Judaism*, 212.

ancient credo that is situated as the culmination of the Hexateuch.[10] The meeting at Shechem over which Joshua presides is set canonically just as Israel is situated in the land. Joshua 1–12 concerns control of the land, albeit by violence, and Joshua 13–21 concerns division of the land among the tribes. I read this moment as Israel's arrival at security, well-being, affluence, and rare self-congratulations. The text is presented as a *bid to non-Israelites* to join up.[11] I shall consider that a fictional staging, so that the text is in fact a *bid to Israelites* in their new affluence to re-embrace the faith of the Yahwistic covenant. The text (and Joshua) know that there are indeed attractive alternatives, alternatives that Israel must resist.

As von Rad saw most clearly, Josh 24:2–13 is a recital of Israel's core memory.[12] It includes the ancestors of Genesis (vv. 2–4), the Exodus (vv. 5–7a), the wilderness sojourn (v. 7b), and the entry into the land (vv. 8–13). This last theme ends: "I gave you a land on which you had not labored, and towns that you had not built, and you live in them; you eat the fruit of vineyards and oliveyards that you did not plant" (v. 13). It is all gift!

After this recital, the speaker (here Joshua the preacher) makes his bid for allegiance to this particular narrative construal of reality: "fear and serve Yahweh in completeness and in faithfulness." Negatively: "put away the other gods." Positively: "serve Yahweh." *Choose:* If Yahweh . . . if not then, Option A is the gods of the Euphrates valley, Option B is the Amorite gods in the land. Choose! Then says the preacher, "those in my household will serve Yahweh," and will put our lives down in the Yahweh narrative just recited. But if you refuse this narrative, then put your life down somewhere else and live with the consequences. No doubt the entire Hexateuch has been pointed to this moment. The Pentateuch consists of the live

---

10. Von Rad, to be sure, takes chapter 24 to be an early credo and Josh 21:43–45 to be the culmination of the Hexateuch (*The Problem of the Hexateuch and Other Essays*, 73–74, 96). The placement of chapter 24, however, is important to the argument concerning its significance, even if he regards it as early.

11. See Brueggemann, *Biblical Perspectives on Evangelism*, 48–70.

12. Von Rad, *The Problem of the Hexateuch*, 6–7.

narrative of Yahweh that generates a world of gift and liberation and demand about which decisions must be made.[13]

Then follows in vv. 16–24 a dialogue about church growth. The exchange of Joshua and the community is a negotiation about the *either/or*.

> **People** (vv. 16–18): Far be us from us to serve other gods . . . we will serve Yahweh;[14]
>
> **Joshua** (vv. 19–20): You cannot do it. It is too hard and Yahweh is more ferocious than you imagine (no growth seduction here).
>
> **People** (v. 21): No, we are committed. We will serve Yahweh.
>
> **Joshua** (v. 22a): You are witnesses . . . you are on notice.
>
> **People** (v. 22b): Yes we are.
>
> **Joshua** (v. 23): with an imperative:
>
> *Negative*: put away foreign gods.[15]
>
> *Positive*: extend your hearts to Yahweh.
>
> *Conclusion* (v. 25): Joshua made a covenant with Torah demands.

This particular crisis of *either/or* is negotiated, and Israel comes to be, yet again, an intentional alternative community, alternative to the gods of the land.

---

13. On narratives producing worlds, see Wilder, "Story and Story-World."

14. The term "far be it from" is an exceedingly strong expression, suggesting the complete inappropriateness of the action, for such an action would profane and render its subject unworthy. See a usage with reference to Yahweh's own action in Gen 18:25.

15. On this negative command, see the parallel in Gen 35:1–4. Some scholars, following Albrecht Alt, suggest that a ritual performance is here envisioned whereby the foreign gods are dramatically banished from the community.

Deutero-Isaiah

The second case of *either/or* that I cite is in Deutero-Isaiah. This wondrous text is situated in the exile. That is, the context is exactly the opposite of Joshua 24. There it was excessive security in the land. Here it is complete displacement from the religious, cultural supports of Jerusalem, set down in an ocean of Babylonian seductions and intimidations, with effective Babylonian economics and seemingly effective Babylonian gods. No doubt many deported Jews found it easier to be a Babylonian Jew, and for some that status was only a transition to becoming Babylonian. The lean choice of remaining Jews embedded in Yahweh depended upon having the *either/or* made plain, for without the *either/or*, cultural accommodation and assimilation go unchecked.

It is precisely the work of Deutero-Isaiah to state the alternative so that Jews tempted by Babylon have a real choice available to them. The text of Deutero-Isaiah is well known to us (unfortunately Handel reworked it so that the *either/or* is not at all visible). The recurring accent of Deutero-Isaiah is that it is now the emergency moment when Jews may and must depart Babylon. In our historical criticism, we have focused much on Cyrus and the overturn of Babylon by the Persians, so that the emancipation of the Jews is a geo-political event. No doubt there is something in that. But I suggest not so much, because the primal departure from Babylon is not geographical, but imaginative, liturgical, and emotional: imagine Jewishness, imagine distinctiveness that has not succumbed to the pressures and seductions of the empire. From this familiar poetry of departure and distinctiveness, I will mention four characteristic elements.

1. The initial announcement, "Comfort, comfort" (Isa 40:1), is an assertion to Jews displaced by Yahweh's anger that caring embrace by Yahweh is now the order of the day: "For a brief moment I abandoned you, but with great compassion I will gather you" (54:7). The Jews in exile are addressed as the forgiven, as the welcomed, as the cherished. They had pondered, for two generations, rejection by Yahweh. But to be forgiven, welcomed, and cherished invites the re-embrace of Jewishness. The poet, moreover, draws out the scenario

of wondrous, jubilant, victorious procession back to Jerusalem, back to Jewishness, back to alternative identity (40:3–8). It is in this reassertion and reenactment of Jewishness that the glory of Yahweh is revealed before all flesh. These Jews in this uncommon identity, moreover, are surrounded by the God who leads like a triumphant general and the God who does the rearguard pickup in order to salvage the dropouts:

> See, the Lord Yahweh comes with might,
> and his arm rules for him . . .
> He will feed his flock like a shepherd;
> he will gather the lambs in his arms,
> and carry them in his bosom,
> and gently lead the mother sheep. (Isa 40:10–11)

The purpose of the poetic opener is to permit the community to re-experience the embracive quality of Jewishness welcomed in its peculiarity.

2. In order to create imaginative space for Jewishness, the poet employs two kinds of rhetorical strategies.[16] First, it is important to debunk the vaunted powers of Babylon. This is done by teasing and mocking the gods of the empire. In Isa 46:1–2, the gods are mocked as dumb statues that must be carried around on the backs of animals, like so many meaningless floats in a May Day parade. The ridicule is like the old humor at the chiefs of the Soviet Union or the mocking of "whitey" that Black people have had do for their own health and sanity. Or the poet holds a mock trial in order to show how weak and ineffectual are the imperial gods who are passive, silent, dormant—all failures who can do neither good nor evil (Isa 41:21–29). The intention of such speech is to dress down the powers of domination, to exhibit courage in the face of power, to show that the choice of Babylon that looks so impressive is in the end sheer foolishness.

3. This debunking is matched by the vigorous reassertion of Yahweh as the most reliable player in the struggle for the future. In

---

16. The fundamental rhetorical analysis is that of Westermann, "Sprache und Struktur der Prophetie Deuterojesajas."

the salvation oracles, this poet has Yahweh repeatedly say to terrified Jews, "fear not." "Fear not, I am with you." "Fear not, I will help you." "Fear not," be a Jew. The poet knows that the empire traffics in fear and intimidation with its uniforms, its parades, its limousines, its press conferences, its agents with dark glasses, and its intrusions in the night. All is for nought, because Yahweh is the great Equalizer who creates safe space and overrides the threat of dominant claims.

4. Finally, looking back on the highway of Isaiah 40 and the fearless safe return that the dumb Babylonian gods cannot stop— nothing can stop resolved Jewishness— the poem announces the departure: "Depart, depart, go out from there" (Isa 52:11)! They could remember the ancient "departure" from Egypt. They remembered every Passover by means of unleavened bread. The lack of leavening recalled that they left in a hurry, with no time for the yeast to rise. This is a like emergency and a like departure. Except,

> For you shall not go out in haste,
>   and you shall not go in flight;
> for Yahweh will go before you,
>   and the God of Israel will be your rear guard. (Isa 52:12)

No rush. Leave at your convenience. First-class passengers may board at their leisure for the journey back to full, alternative Jewishness: "For you shall go out in joy, and be led back in peace" (Isa 55:12).

They might not depart the emotional grip of Babylon on the day they first hear the poem; but the poetry lingers. Alternative identity, even in places of threat and seduction, is embraced as the invitation does its proper work.

The Courageous Utterances of Witnesses

The *either/or* of distinctive identity for praise and obedience is not self-evident in the nature of things, but *depends completely and exclusively upon the courageous utterance of witnesses who voice choices and invite decisions where none were self-evident.* My accent on the urgency of preaching the *either/or* is grounded in my conviction that Israel lives by a certain kind of utterance without which

9

Israel has no chance to live. It is for this reason that I have insisted in my recent book on Old Testament theology that Old Testament claims for God finally do not appeal to historical facticity or to ontology, but rely upon the utterance of witnesses to offer what is not self-evident or otherwise available.[17] This is indeed "theology of the word," by which I mean simply and leanly and crucially *utterance.*

I take as my primary case Deutero-Isaiah, admittedly an easy case; but I would extrapolate from Deutero-Isaiah to claim the entire Old Testament is utterance that expresses *either/or* that is not self-evident.[18] The massive hegemony of Babylon—political, economic, theological—had, so far as we know, well nigh driven Jewishness from the horizon; and with the elimination of Jewishness it had vetoed Yahweh from the theological conversation. It is the intention of every hegemony to eliminate separatist construals of reality that are endlessly inconvenient and problematic, and certainly a separatism as dangerous as Jewishness that endlessly subverts. The tale of Daniel, perhaps later but clearly reflective of the Babylonian crisis, tells the tale of how Nebuchadnezzar is enraged that Jews should refuse imperial allegiance and hold to their odd alternative claim (Dan 3:13–15).

This power of hegemony, moreover, matched the exiles' own sense of things, for they also had concluded that Yahweh was not engaged or worth trusting:

> Why do you say, O Jacob,
> and speak, O Israel,
> "My way is hidden from Yahweh,
> and my right is disregarded by my God"? (40:27)

> But Zion said, "Yahweh has forsaken me,
> my Lord has forgotten me." (49:14)

---

17. See Brueggemann, *Theology of the Old Testament,* 117–44.

18. It is evident that "testimony" is a way to make a claim from "below," when one lacks the tools and authority to make a more established sort of claim for truth. See my comments on Ricoeur and Wiesel in *Theology of the Old Testament.*

> Is my hand shortened, that I cannot redeem?
> Or have I no power to deliver? (50:2)

It is in such an environment of hegemony-*cum*-despair that the utterance of *either/or* takes place. It is the utterance of *either/or* that shapes the perceptual field of Israel anew, to become aware of resources not recognized, of dangers not acknowledged, and of choices that had not seemed available. I shall consider this new, subversive voice of *either/or* in two waves. First, Deutero-Isaiah himself, perhaps someone who had arisen out of a continuing seminar on the text of First Isaiah, is now moved to generate and extrapolate new text. "Moved," I say, because some think it was by an out-of-the-ordinary confrontation in "the divine council": when the voices say "Cry . . . what shall I cry . . . get you up on a high mountain, herald of good tidings," the one moved by divine imperative is none other than Deutero-Isaiah, who moves out from this theological experience to reshape the lived emergency of Israel.

It is this poet who gives to the rhetoric of the synagogue and church the term "gospel."[19] Indeed, I suggest provisionally that gospel is the offer of an *either/or* where none seemed available. So in Isa 40:9:

> Get you up to a high mountain,
>   O Zion, herald of *gospel tidings*,
> lift up your voice with strength,
>   O Jerusalem, herald of *gospel tidings*,
> lift it up, do not fear.

The gospeler is twice named. The gospeler, moreover, is given the utterance to be sounded: "Behold, your God," or in NRSV, "Here is your God." It is the exhibit of Yahweh as God of the exiles in a context where Babylon had banished the God of the exiles so that there were only Babylonian gods available. The news is that Yahweh is back in play, creating choices. Yahweh is back in play on the lips of the one moved to new utterance.

That text in 40:9 is matched in 52:7 in a better known utterance:

---

19. See Brueggemann, *Biblical Perspectives on Evangelism*, especially 26–30.

> How beautiful upon the mountains
>> are the feet of the *gospel messenger* who announces peace,
> who brings *gospel news*,
>> who announces salvation,
>> who says to Zion, "Your God reigns."

Again the term gospel is twice used, and again the lines are given: "Your God reigns," or better, "Your God has just become king." The line is a quote from the Psalms (see 96:10), but the utterance here is an assertion that in the contest for domination, the gods of the empire have been defeated and the God of Israel is now the dominant force in creation. The poet creates an environment for choice, for decision, for homecoming, for new, faithful action, none of which is available or choosable without this utterance.

It is, however, the second layer of utterance in this poetry that interests me, namely that the Jews in exile are summoned by the poet to be witnesses, to give testimony about the Yahwistic alternative about which they did not know and which the Babylonians certainly could never tolerate. In Isa 43:8–13, the poet offers a contest among the gods. Negatively he invites the Babylonians to give evidence for their gods: "Let them bring forth their witnesses" (v. 9). Then in v. 10: "You are my witnesses," you exiles. You are the ones who are to speak my name, confess my authority, obey my will, accept my emancipation, tell my miracles. The exiles who themselves had thought there was no *or* to the Babylonian *either* are now called to testify to this Yahwistic *or*. There are two quite remarkable features to this poem authorizing Israel's testimonial utterance about an alternative that the empire cannot tolerate.

First, the summons and authorization to testify is interwoven with *the substance of testimony* that is to be given:

> Before me no god was formed,
>> nor shall there be any after me.
> I, I am Yahweh,
>> and besides me there is no savior . . .
> I am God, and also henceforth I am He;
>> there is no one who can deliver from my hand;
>> I work and who can hinder it? (43:10b–11, 13)

What is to be said is that Yahweh is the alpha and the omega, the first and the last, the creator, the one who is utterly irresistible. Note well that this extravagant claim allows no room for any Babylonian gods. In the statement of the *either/or*, the Babylonian *either* is dismissed as an irrelevant fantasy. There is only the Yahwistic *or* as an option. Now we might suspect that this is a frontal assault to convince the Babylonians. Perhaps so. But the second feature I observe in v. 10 is this:

> You are my witnesses, says Yahweh,
>   and my servant whom I have chosen,
> so that you may know and believe me
>   and understand that I am he.

Notice: You are my witnesses . . . in order that . . . *you may know, believe, understand!*

The giving of testimony is to claim the ones who testify. Israel is to enunciate the Yahwistic option so that they themselves should trust and embrace that option. This is surely the most direct claim I know concerning Paul's assertion that faith comes from what is heard (Rom 10:17); where there is no speaking and hearing of an alternative world, there is no faith, no courage, no freedom to choose differently, no community of faith apart from and even against the empire.

The other remarkable text is Isa 44:8, followed by the negative of 44:9. It is clear that vv. 8 and 9 belong to quite different literary units; they are joined together perhaps to make the point about utterance. Verse 8 asserts yet again, "You are my witnesses." The last two lines of the verse, just as we have seen in chapter 43, outline the utterance that is to be uttered:

> Is there any god besides me?
>   There is no other rock; I know not one.

The testimony is that there is not only a choice outside Babylon. It is the only real choice. The new feature here, after chapter 43, is the first line of the verse to the witnesses now being recruited: "Do not fear, or be afraid." One can imagine a lawyer briefing a witness, perhaps a witness who is a whistleblower against a great corpora-tion, who must say in court what the company cannot tolerate: "Do not be afraid." Or one can imagine a women in a rape trial who must give evidence, but is terrified both of the shame and of the continu-ing threat of the rapist: "Do not fear." The lawyer must encourage and reassure. Every witness, every serious preacher, every exile who speaks against hegemony knows the fear. And Yahweh says, state the *or*, because it is true. Many witnesses discover, of course, that Yahweh in the end has no "witness protection program," but the witness is often compelled to give evidence nonetheless.

The negative of v. 9 is surprising. Verses 9–20 constitute an odd unit that mocks the makers of idols, the Babylonians who manufacture powerless gods. Verse 9 speaks of idols and then of witnesses, that is, the Babylonian gods and the Babylonians who champion them or Jews who trust those imperial gods too much. The idols are, with the NRSV, "nothing." The term looks like a sim-ple rejection. But the Hebrew *tohu* = chaos. The Babylonian gods are embodiments of chaos, forces of disorder. This is a remarkable claim, for the empire had claimed to be a great sponsor of order and well-being. But here it is clear: the spiritual force of the empire is against *shalom*, against peace and order and well-being. The *tohu* of Babylon of course is to be contrasted with the power of the true creator God, Yahweh. Finally it is asserted that the witnesses who champion the gods of *tohu* neither see nor know. They are so nar-coticized and mesmerized by the empire that they cannot see what is going on. The contrast is total, no overlap between these two god offers. The exiles can choose either *the gods of the empire* who will never deliver the well-being they claim to sponsor, or *the God of the news* who stands against all things fearful. The battle for Jewishness in exile is acute, a battle now replicated in the battle for baptism in an ocean of military consumerism that generates endless layers of chaos in the name of prosperity.

To be sure, Deutero-Isaiah is an easy case for *either/or* through utterance. But I would argue that the theme is pervasive in the text of this people always struggling for its identity. Perhaps you noticed in my longish comment on Joshua 24 that Joshua and his coun-terparts finally get serious precisely about testimony. He says to them: "You are witnesses against yourselves that you have chosen Yahweh, to serve him" (v. 22). The answer, "Witnesses." The Hebrew is terse, without a nominative pronoun. My point is a simple one. Everything depends upon utterance. The dramatic occasions of teaching and preaching where the *either/or* is spelled out and sometimes embraced, are serious occasions, serious not simply because of formal oath or because we claim to be speaking true, but serious elementally because *what we say* and *how we say* is the world we receive. Israel's serious oath is to choose the *or* of Yahweh and to hold to it (see also Josh 24:27).

It would be nice if the *either/or* were simply out there in the landscape. Israel, however, knows better. It is here, in speech. If it is not uttered, it is not available. If it is not uttered, it is not. This point, that human possibility resides in utterance, it seems to me, is crucial not only for preaching, but more generally in a technological society.[20] Our technological mindset wants to thin, reduce, and eventually silence serious speech. The urgency of preaching and all the utterance of the church and the synagogue, I suggest, is that we know intuitively that where there is not face-to-face truth-telling, we are by that much diminished in the human enterprise. And, Joshua insists, Israel must stand by its utterance.[21]

At Hand, but Not Yet

While the *either/or* may be uttered frontally, *the or of Yahweh is characteristically spoken in figure*, because it is a possibility "at hand" but not yet in hand.[22] The *either/or* of Yahwism is directly utterable, and I have cited cases of such direct utterance. Characteristically, however, it is not done tersely and confrontationally, because such

20. The most fundamental analysis is that of Ellul, *Technological Society*; see more specifically to our point, Ellul, *The Humiliation of the Word*.

21. On the integrity of speech and matching speech to life, see Berry, *Standing by Words*, 24–63.

22. In recent time, Paul Ricoeur has understood most clearly and most consistently that serious religious language must be spoken in "figure," thus his accent on imagination. Speech that is not in "figure" runs the prompt risk of idolatry, of producing what can be controlled. See the several essays in his book nicely titled, *Figuring the Sacred: Religion, Narrative, and Imagination*.

utterance is too lean, gives the listeners few resources for the tricky negotiation between options, and because the *either/or*, having no one shape or form, is always different with different folk in different circumstance. Moreover, while the *either* of hegemony is visible and can be described in some detail, the *or* of Yahweh does not admit of flat description because it is not yet visible, not yet in hand, always about to be, always under construal, always just beyond us. Indeed, if the *or* of Yahweh could be fully and exhaustively described, the prospect is that it would become, almost immediately, some new hegemonic *either*, as is often the case if creeds are heard too flatly, if liturgies are held too closely, if ethics is turned to legalism, if piety becomes self-confidence and pride. It is this open act of imagination in the service of a demanding, healing *or* that is the primary hard work of the preacher and the wonder of good preaching that is communicated in modes outside hegemonic certitude.

I will return to my two major cases and then in conclusion note three other places where one can see some playfulness at work in utterance.

1. I have characterized Joshua 24 as a primary model of *either/or* in which testimonial utterance is evident. That utterance of either/or in solemn assembly by Joshua culminates in v. 25: "So Joshua made a covenant with the people that day, and made statutes and ordinances for them at Shechem." The verse tells us almost nothing of what constitutes the new obedience to which Israel is pledged after this hard-won decision to embrace Yahweh's *or.* I suggest that because Joshua 24 is about the immediate settlement in the land, the Torah of Deuteronomy is the figurative articulation that fleshes out the *either/or* announced in Joshua 24. For the sake of that connection, I make two critical observations. First, it is generally agreed that Deuteronomy constitutes the norm for the "history" offered in Joshua, Judges, Samuel, and Kings, the "Deuteronomic" account of Israel's life in the land.[23] Thus the linkage between Deuteronomy and Joshua 24 is entirely plausible; Josh 24:25 alludes to that Torah. Second, because Deuteronomy is "Deuteronomic," we are free to say that its framing is fictive, that the staging of the speech of Moses

---

23. See a summary of this scholarship by Fretheim, *Deuteronomic History.*

at the Jordan is an invitation for Israel that has embraced the Yahwistic *or* against the Canaanite *either* to conjure what the land of
promise would be like were it alternatively organized and practiced
in covenant. This delivers us from needing to insist that Israel enacted all these laws; but it also permits us to see the "laws" as acts of
imagination in which each successive generation of *or* is to explore
how to take this text into its own concrete life and practice.

I shall comment on three texts from Deuteronomy. The ones
I have selected are perhaps easy cases, but the point will be more
generally clear. Joshua counts on the clear *either/or* worked out in
detail by Moses.

1. *Either* let the economy work unfettered so that the rich become richer, or read Deut 15:1–18 on the "Year of Release."²⁴ Moses,
in this text, anticipates and imagines that the economy of the land
of Canaan does not need to be organized in exploitative "Canaanite" ways, but could be reorganized in neighborly Israelite ways. He
offers a scenario for a society in which poor people must work off
their debts (no doubt at high interest rates), but a neighborly ethic
proposes that at the end of six years, the debt is canceled and the
poor person is invited back into the economy.

—Moses said, there will always be poor people, so you must take
 this seriously and keep doing it all the time (v. 11).

—Moses said, if you do it effectively, you can eliminate such de-
 meaning poverty and "the poor will cease out of the land"
 (v. 4).

—Moses said, "Do not entertain mean thoughts and begin to
 count toward the seventh year and act in hostility" (v. 9).

—Moses said, do not only cancel the debt but give the poor a
 generous stake so that they can re-enter the economy vi-
 ably, not from the bottom up (vv. 7–10).

—Moses said, if this seems outrageous to you, remember that
 you were bond-servants in Egypt, and you were released

24. On this pivotal command, see Hamilton, *Social Justice and Deuteronomy*.

by the generous power of Yahweh your redeemer who
brought you out (v. 18).

This is the most radical *or* in the Bible, insisting that the
economy must be embedded in a neighborly human fabric. Almost
all of us choose the *either*, imagining that Joshua's *or* is not relevant
to an urban, post-industrial economy. But there it sits, always a
summons, always a reminder, always an invitation. And Joshua had
already said, "I tried to talk you out of this *or*, I told you it was too
difficult for you."

2. *Either* let legitimate authority run loose in self-serving acquisitiveness, *or* read Deut 17:14–20 on monarchy. It is the only law
of Moses on kingship. Moses agrees only reluctantly to let Israel
have a king; he thought kingship a bad idea and all available models of centralized power were bad. Then he says: but if you must,
your king—your Israelite, covenantal, neighborly king—shall be
different. This king, embedded in covenant, must not accumulate
silver or gold or horses or chariots or wives. Moses knows the three
great seductions are money, power, and sex, all of which make community impossible if they are accumulated. And so he offers an *or*.
The king, when in office, shall sit all day, every day, reading Torah,
meditating day and night on what Yahweh intends, on how covenantal community can curb raw power.

Israel, like every government since, has found it difficult to
choose this *or*. The kings of Israel characteristically took the *either* of
raw power, as has every kind of power . . . priests, parents, teachers,
deans, bishops, corporate executives. In Israel, the primal example
of the power of greed is Solomon: gold, gold, gold, 300 wives, 700
concubines; and later it was said, "Do not be anxious, even Solomon in all his vast royal apparatus was not as well off as a bird" (see
Matt 6:28–29).[25] The *or* is about power and governance and greed.
In the end, however, it is about anxiety, getting more, keeping more
while the land is lost in dread, terror, and devouring.[26]

25. See Brueggemann, "Faith with a Price."

26. The "or" of covenantal power is nicely put in the words of Jesus in Mark
10:42–44.

3. *Either* it is every man [sic] for himself at the expense of all the others, *or* read Deut 24:19–22. It is about the triangle of *land-owner, land,* and *landless,* and how they will live together. The *either* of Canaanite agriculture is just a "labor pool" of those nameless ones without any leverage or fringe benefits, who work but fall farther and farther behind, until they drop into welfare and then out of welfare into drugs, alcohol, sometimes a threat to us, often an inconvenience, always a nuisance and embarrassment. *Or,* says Moses, in your economic operations, leave enough for *the alien, the widow, the orphan.* Leave the sheaves of wheat when you are "bringing in the sheaves," for *the alien, the widow, the orphan.* When you beat your olive trees, leave enough for *the alien, the widow, the orphan.* When you gather grapes, leave some for *the alien, the widow, the orphan.* The triad is like a mantra for this *or* of covenant because Moses knows that the powerful are in common destiny with the powerless. The haves are linked to the future of the have-nots. Moses had already said, "Same law for citizens and undocumented workers" (Lev 19:34). Moses knew that in a patriarchal society women without husbands and children without fathers are lost to the community, as bad off as outsiders.

The *or* requires a break with the orthodoxy of individualism. It requires a rejection of the notion of the undeserving poor. It requires a negation of all the pet ideologies whereby unburdened freedom is the capacity to disregard neighbor. And it is all there in the deep command of Yahweh . . . not socialism, not liberalism, not ideology, just an alternative life.[27]

Our Christian strategy for disposing of the Mosaic is to dismiss it as legalism, certain we are justified by grace alone, except that this obedience belongs to the center of an alternative community. The *or* is demanding but not obvious. The mantra of this community is endlessly "love God, then love neighbor, neighbor, neighbor."

2. I have characterized Isaiah 40–55 as a primary model of *either/or* testimonial utterance for this special community almost succumbing to Babylon. It was to this little community without

---

27. On neighborliness extended to outsiders and the weak insiders, see Luke 4:26–27.

confidence and almost without conviction that the poet declared on Yahweh's behalf:

> because you are precious in my sight,
>> and honored, and I love you,
> I give people in return for you,
>> nations in exchange for your life. (Isa 43:4)

Deutero-Isaiah, however, only provides the trigger for liturgical, emotional, imaginative, perhaps geographical homecoming. When the Jews did come back to Jerusalem in 537 or 520 or 444, Deutero-Isaiah gave little guidance. But then, Deutero-Isaiah never comes without Trito-Isaiah. I propose that Trito-Isaiah (Isaiah 56–66) is the figurative articulation that fleshes out the *either/or* of Deutero-Isaiah.[28] There is now a great deal of ferment about the book of Isaiah. It is increasingly likely, in scholarly judgment, that the old, deep separation of Deutero- and Trito-Isaiah cannot be sustained. And therefore in its canonical shaping, one may see Isaiah 56–66 as an attempt to enact the glorious vision of Deutero-Isaiah; but enactments must always come to detail.

1. *Either* be a community of like-minded people who are convinced of their own purity, virtue, orthodoxy, and legitimacy, excluding all others, *or* read Isa 56:3–8. There were all around the edges of restored Judaism inconvenient people who had no claim to purity, virtue, orthodoxy, or legitimacy. There were late-comers, not good Jews with pedigrees, who had joined in, drawn to the faith— perhaps Samaritans or whatever, but surely not "qualified." Worse than that, there were people with marked, scarred, compromised genitals, people who had sold out to Babylon in order to become willing eunuchs with access to power. Of these Moses long ago in Deut 23:1 had declared that people with irregular sexual disposition were excluded. It is there in the Torah. All around were hovering people not like us, claiming and pushing and yearning and even believing . . . What to do?

Says the *or* of Trito-Isaiah: have a generous spirit and a minimum but clear bar of admission. Tilt toward inclusiveness with only

---

28. See Emmerson, *Isaiah 56–66*; and Achtemeier, *The Community and Message of Isaiah 56–66*.

two requirements: that they keep covenant, that is submit to the neighborly intention of Yahweh; that they keep sabbath, rest from the madness of production and consumption as a sign of confidence in Yahweh's governance. That's all! It is the *or* of inclusiveness, no other pedigree, no sexual transposition, no other purification, an *or* that says the community is not made in the image of our strong points. The community teems with people who score irregularly on every Myers-Briggs notion of how we are and how we ought to be.[29]

2. *Either* become a punctilious community of religious discipline, engaging in religious scruple with amazing callousness about the real world of human transaction, *or* read Isa 58:1–9 and consider an alternative religious discipline of fasting that is not for show or piety or self-congratulations. Practice fast that commits to the neighbor, specifically the neighbor in need, the neighbor boxed in injustice and oppression. Break the vicious cycles of haves and have-nots that produce hungry people and homeless people and naked people, the most elemental signs and gestures of exposure, vulnerability, and degradation, produced by a system that does not notice.

Conventional religious disciplines that feel like virtue are disconnected. The practitioners of such self-congratulation, all the while, exploit and oppress and quarrel; they are uncaring, unthinking, unnoticing. And now the *or* of engagement moves to solidarity with the exposed and the vulnerable. The NRSV says "they are your kin," but the Hebrew says "flesh," your own flesh of flesh and bone of bone, self of self. That is who they are.

When the lines of separation between haves and have-nots are broken by true fast, then, says Trito-Isaiah, then, only then, not until then:

> *Then* your light shall break forth like the dawn,
> and your healing shall spring up quickly;
> your vindicator shall go before you,
> the glory of Yahweh shall be your rear guard.

---

29. The New Testament counterpart to such "foreigners and eunuchs" is perhaps "publicans and sinners," on which see Mark 2:15–17.

> *Then* you shall call, and Yahweh will answer;
> you shall cry for help, and he will say, "Here I am." (58:8–9)

Then, then, then, then . . . it is the *or* of communion. There is, however, no communion with Yahweh until there is community with neighbor.[30]

3. *Either* cling to the old status quo of social arrangements and miss God's newness, *or* read Isa 65:17–25. The *or* of poetic imagination asserts that the old heaven and the old earth and the old Jerusalem, the old holy city and every old holy city and every old city and every old power arrangement is on the way out and is being displaced. The *or* of world renewal and urban renewal is a fantasy. The community of *or* engages in a strong act of vision: "We have a dream." It is a dream of joy and well-being; a dream in which there are no more cries of distress, no more infant mortality, no more social dislocation when people build houses and lose them due to taxation, war, ethnic cleansing, or Olympic committees; where people do not plant gardens and have to move before harvest time. In the world coming there is no more anguish in childbirth. And to top it all, there is reconciliation of creation, lions and lambs, immediate communion with and attentiveness from Yahweh who answers before we call.

The poet offers a breathtaking *or.* He has been radical in Isaiah 56 on eunuchs and 58 on poor people. But now in chapter 65 he no longer has time for the conventions of reality as he is off on a poetic, evangelical fantasy of what might be and what will be and what is at hand, but not in hand. He imagines, against the lovers of the old city who had felt but not yet noticed the brutal dysfunction of the old city. All will be changed. The poet can scarcely see its shape, but he has no doubt that its coming shape is a healing of all old abrasions and despairs. This *or* will never happen among us while we are bound to what was. Thus the poem is more like a parable than a blueprint, but a parable to be ingested by reforming Judaism, a parable,

- about a banquet

30. On neighborly attentiveness as a condition of well-being, see Matt 25:31–46.

- about a rich man and a barn
- about a man with two sons
- about a neighborly foreigner who paid the bills
- about a nagging widow
- about day laborers who get full pay.[31]

None of that is visible yet. Indeed none of that is possible . . . yet—except for those who depart the way things are for the One who will make things new.

Foolish and Urgent

I am taking an ecclesial agenda because for too long, so it seems to me, christological certitude in the church has much of the time been permitted to silence, trump, and give closure to the Old Testament. I have wanted to suggest that faithful Christian exposition could do otherwise. I regard the preacher's engagement with the Old Testament as urgent:

—because the *or* of faith, so deeply pondered by ancient Israel, is needed in the face of our dominant *either*;

—because in a technological society, it is mostly left to the preacher, who labors at it locally, to voice the human options in a crisis of flatness;

—because preachers, more than any others, have endless opportunity for the tease of detail whereby the *or* of the gospel may be received and embraced.

The *or* is an impossible possibility. Both Israel and the church have always known that. That is what makes preaching both foolish and urgent.

---

31. Among the most helpful treatments of the parables is Donahue, *The Gospel in Parable.* See also Scott, *Hear Then the Parable*; and Herzog, *Parables as Subversive Speech.*

2

Advent

Departure and Homecoming

ADVENT, MORE THAN ANY other season in the church year, is most powerfully contradicted by the socioeconomic practices of our society. That is why Advent preaching is so difficult and why we are temped to cheat and slide over into Christmas as soon as we can. It is exceedingly difficult to live in the tension and maintain the tension between Advent and "early Christmas" in a consumer culture.

In fact, Advent still belongs to the Old Testament and is preoccupied with the hopes of Israel that have not yet come to fruition. There is a *waiting* that is required, and a summons to wait with *discipline*. But our Advent preaching must be done in a culture of instant gratification that wants to wait for nothing, a self-indulgent culture that resists any inconvenient discipline. The consumer orgy that has come to dominate Christmas shopping is the most vulgar form of "realized eschatology"; it imagines *we have it all now*. Consequently, there is nothing yet to receive and nothing for which to hope. But Advent is the insistence that "coming soon" is the great "plus" of the newness that is "at hand" but not yet visible. In the church season, there is a wait until Christmas, for the time when "the wondrous gift is given." In Advent that wondrous gift is "at hand" . . . but not yet in hand. Thus I suggest that Advent preaching is about *hope* in a culture that attempts to fend off its despair by frantic self-indulgent busyness that is determined to work itself into a frazzle; that frazzle serves: a) to keep us from hoping; and b) to keep us from the hopelessness that saturates our common polity.

Advent as Changed Subject

The Old Testament/Hebrew Bible is a Book of Hope that has received various fulfillments in Jewish and Christian tradition. In a notorious way, Rudolf Bultmann has argued, from an acute christological stance, that by itself the Old Testament does not reach fulfillment, i.e., that it awaits Jesus. It is true that the Old Testament awaits fulfillment, though one need not (and must not) cast that reality in Bultmann's supersessionist terms. We may do better to pay attention to the ending of the Old Testament/Hebrew Bible as it is given in two quite different shapes.

On the one hand, the Jews have a particular ordering for the Hebrew canon, and it ends with 1 and 2 Chronicles, culminating with the decree of the Persian ruler, Cyrus:

> In the first year of King Cyrus of Persia, in fulfillment of the word of Yahweh spoken by Jeremiah, Yahweh stirred up the spirit of King Cyrus of Persia so that he sent a herald throughout all his kingdom and also declared in a written edict: "Thus says King Cyrus of Persia: Yahweh, the God of heaven, has given me all the kingdoms of the earth, and he has charged me to build him a house at Jerusalem, which is in Judah. Whoever is among you of all his people, may Yahweh his God be with him! Let him go up." (2 Chron 36:22–23)

It is noteworthy, in passing, that even the decree of the foreign ruler is linked to prophetic hope in an allusion to Jer 50:9, a connection that subsumes even imperial policies under the rule of Yahweh.[1]

---

1. The verb "stir up" is a preferred usage to characterize the undefined way in which God impinges upon the public human process (see Isa 41:2, 25; 45:13; Jer 51:11; Hag 1:14). It is instructive that in the Anglican tradition, two of the four collects for Advent use the verb in an imperative.

In that rendering, the culmination of Jewish Scripture is the permit of Cyrus who has been "stirred up" by Yahweh. That decree allowed displaced Jews to go home and resume life in the territory of Judah, amid Jerusalem. That is a powerful hope that eventuated—through Ezra and Nehemiah—in the restoration movement of Judaism. Of this culminating promise, we may notice four matters:

1. The promise is exclusively for Jews. The restoration of Judaism is the final hope of the text. Indeed, Jon Levenson in his important book has recently connected "resurrection faith" and "God's ultimate victory" to the "restoration of Israel."[2]

2. The hope is a political/historical one made with reference to the political-imperial decision on the part of the Persian empire.

3. The hope is concretely material and concerns land. This sort of promise continues to play in the contemporary state of Israel and in the hope for the re-establishment of Jerusalem. But we should not miss the theological angle: land claims are linked to the larger purpose and will of Yahweh with particular reference to Jews.[3]

4. Perhaps most important, the Hebrew canon culminates with a literature of hope in the Persian period. Indeed Old Testament scholarship is now largely preoccupied with the Persian period of Israel's memory.[4] There are, to be sure, some pieces of literature in the Old Testament that are later than the Persian period in the Hellenistic era. But they are not defining for the hope of Judaism. In the book of Daniel, which is judged critically to be set in the Hellenistic period, moreover, the memory in the text is situated in the time of Nebuchadnezzar in the sixth century. Historical location fixes Jewish hope in the Hebrew Bible to that time and place.

2. Levenson, *Resurrection and the Restoration of Israel.*

3. Brueggemann, *The Land.*

4. Berquist, *Judaism in Persia's Shadow.*

On the other hand, Christians have their own ordering for the books of the Old Testament, which enunciate a very different hope in its conclusion. I have noted the Cyrus decree in 2 Chron 36:22–23 because I have wanted to contrast that final articulation of hope with the final hope voiced in the Christian Old Testament in Mal 4:5–6. It is of enormous significance that the Hebrew Bible ends in *imperial decree,* for Jews are always living amid empire; it is equally significant that the Christian Old Testament ends with *a prophetic oracle*, an act of imagination and expectation that is propelled not by political analysis, but by divine promise that surges beyond *Realpolitik.* I do not for an instant suggest that the latter articulation is a superior one, only that it is very different.

The Christian Old Testament ends with a divine promise that Elijah will return with the capacity to reconcile parents and children (Mal 4:5–6). This concluding oracle thus attests that God is not finished, that God intends reconciliation in time to come, and that God will authorize human agency (Elijah) to accomplish that reconciliation. We may read the Elijah promise backward and forward.

When we read the Elijah promise back to 1 Kings 17–21, we arrive at this narrative character who had the courage and authority to challenge kings, override death, evoke rain, and make all things new. He is an uncredentialed agent who subverts royal authority and puts his authority to work against the rapacious policies of establishment economics. It is astonishing that the Old Testament ends with a divine assurance that this unsettling, subversive agent will reappear in time to come in order to overcome the alienations of family and society. (The Jews as well, at Passover, anticipate the coming again of Elijah.)

When we read this promise forward into the New Testament, we arrive at John the Baptist who is the key character in the drama of Advent and the last character in the Old Testament. The gospel writers do not spend much energy linking John to Elijah, but the connection is quite explicit in Luke 1:8–17 where the angel announces the birth of John: "With the spirit and power of Elijah he will go before him, to turn the hearts of parents to their children, and the disobedient to the wisdom of the righteous, to make ready a people prepared for the Lord" (Luke 1:17).

In this part of the angelic enunciation, there is a direct allusion to the promise of Malachi, but that promise is now expanded in explicit ways. John, soon to be born,

—will turn the hearts of parents to the children;

—will turn the disobedient to the wisdom of the righteous; and

—will make ready a people prepared for Yahweh.

The exposition of the Malachi offered by Luke has both modified and extended the expectation in order to draw closer to John.

In addition to this explicit linkage, two Advent texts in this year's common lectionary reference John. In Matt 3:1–12, the Gospel reading for the Second Sunday in Advent, John is described as an uncredentialed outsider who enters into dispute with Jewish leadership (Pharisees and Sadducees). He speaks harsh words of judgment, urges repentance, and dismisses their claims of pedigree. Then he announces the one "coming after me," who will *gather* the wheat and *burn* the chaff. That is, he anticipates one who will sort out who is qualified to be the "new people," the ones prepared, gathered around the new leader.

The second reading is Matt 11:2–11, the Gospel reading for the Third Sunday in Advent, which ends (in verses excluded from the lectionary) that "he is Elijah who is to come" (v. 14). In this narrative account John claims his role as prophet whose work is to proclaim the coming one. John's assertion is in the wake of Jesus' message to him about Jesus as a transformative agent who makes all things new:

> Jesus answered them, "Go and tell John what you hear and see: the blind receive their sight, the lame walk, the lepers are cleansed, the deaf hear, the dead are raised, and the poor have good news brought to them. And blessed is anyone who takes no offense at me." (Matt 11:4–6)

The interface of John and Jesus, so well articulated here, consists in: (a) John's *demanding preparation* and (b) Jesus' *performance of newness*. Clearly the account in Matthew intends that the two,

John and Jesus, prophetic voice and transformative agent, cannot be separated from each other any more than they can be confused with each other. In this rendering, John is the teacher who guides preparation so that "a people prepared" may receive the newness. But the newness of Jesus, reported back to John, is not the news of consumer goods or security or self-indulgence or any of the matters that constitute our usual "Christmas season." Rather the newness that is promised and enacted is the rehabilitation of human well being among the disabled and the disinherited . . . the blind, the lame, the lepers, the deaf, the dead, and the poor. It is as though John, counting on the declaration of Jesus, is seeking to change the subject away from conventional desires to the gifts of the new regime that concern the most elemental human possibilities of health, healing, and wholeness, all of which require wrenching transformation out of old settled conventions. I suggest that Advent preaching might indeed focus on *changing the subject,* away from much of our usual agenda. If we begin with John and read backward (even as Matt 11:2–11 begins with Jesus and reads back to John), we read back to Malachi and the promise of reconciliation; if we read back from Malachi to Elijah, we understand why Elijah is identified as "troubler" in Israel (1 Kgs 18:17) and "my enemy" (1 Kgs 21:20). The force of Elijah's ministry was a huge "trouble" to settled power in Israel. And now John—via Malachi—anticipates the coming time when Jesus comes to heal and transform.

We are able to recall that Jesus' adversaries resisted his healing power. As soon as he healed, they sought to destroy him, because present power arrangements thrive on social relationships of disability that foster fear, anxiety, exploitation, and violence (Mark 3:6). A change of subject toward the gifts of health, healing, and wholeness exposes conventional modes of management as fraudulent and pathological. What Elijah, Malachi, John, and Jesus discovered is that most of their hearers have an enormous stake in the way things are and resent the cost and refuse the disciplines of a changed agenda. What a way to imagine Advent preaching as a changed subject that calls attention to social possibilities that we would rather not notice. Preparation consists in receiving a new agenda, and that cannot happen through conventional busyness that our society practices in order to keep from facing the new agenda.

John the Baptist as Transitional Character

If we take John the Baptist as the key character in Advent and as the last character in the Old Testament, then we may notice one other remarkable matter about John in the narrative. It is this: in all four Gospels, when John announces the coming Messiah, he quotes verses from Isaiah 40:

> This is the one of whom the prophet Isaiah spoke when he said,
> "The voice of one crying out in the wilderness:
> Prepare the way of the Lord,
>> make his paths straight." (Matt 3:3)[5]

> As it is written in the prophet Isaiah,
> "See, I am sending my messenger ahead of you,
>> who will prepare your way;
> the voice of one crying out in the wilderness:
> 'Prepare the way of the Lord,
>> make his paths straight.'" (Mark 1:2–3)

> As it is written in the book of the words of the prophet Isaiah,
> "The voice of one crying out in the wilderness:
> 'Prepare the way of the Lord,
>> make his paths straight.
> Every valley shall be filled,
>> and every mountain and hill shall be made low,
> and the crooked shall be made straight,
>> and the rough ways made smooth;
> and all flesh shall see the salvation of God.'" (Luke 3:4–6)

> He said,
> "I am the voice of one crying out in the wilderness,

5. This text is the Gospel reading for the Second Sunday in Advent.

'Make straight the way of the Lord,'"
as the prophet Isaiah said. (John 1:23)

The quotes from Isaiah 40 serve different purposes in each of these four citations. But given such differences in nuance, it is nonetheless the case that the commonality of quotation is a defining feature of John's message, and so a defining note of Advent.

We may linger a while to ponder why it is that John appealed to these verses, and why it is that the gospel writers all embrace that common memory. What does it mean to have exposition of Jesus drawn into the orbit of Isaiah 40?

Departure and Homecoming

As is well known among us (note Handel's *Messiah*), Isaiah 40 begins the second part of the Book of Isaiah that stands in deep tension with Isaiah 1–29. Isaiah 40 would seem to be an utterance that is situated at the beginning of the Persian Empire under Cyrus (about 540 BCE) and stands historically remote from Isaiah 39 that concluded the first part of the Book of Isaiah. Isaiah 39 concerns Hezekiah and reflects the time about 690 BCE. This means that the time between Isaiah 39 and Isaiah 40 (690 to 540 BCE) is about 150 years. It is as though the faithful have waited 150 years for this poetic utterance. In that 150 years a great deal has happened to the city of Jerusalem on which Isaiah reflects, the destruction of the city and the displacement of its leading inhabitants.

In Isa 39:5–7, the prophet announced that the leading members of the Jerusalem establishment, including members of the royal family, will be carried away into exile. Then, after 150 years of silence and waiting, the Isaiah tradition speaks again to announce a homecoming to those who have been displaced as exiles. The poetry of Isa 40:1–11 purports to be a decision made in the heavenly realm of the gods about the deployment of new political reality on earth. The text:

- asserts God's pardon for punished Jerusalem (vv. 1–2);

- imagines a highway that will permit displaced Jews to return home in splendor (vv. 3–4);

- asserts that God's promissory word is reliable (vv. 8–9);

- commissions a messenger to announce "gospel news" to those who have been displaced (v. 9);

- offers a summary of the good news, "Here is your God" (v. 9);

- presents God as the protector on the journey home, God as powerful warrior, God as gentle shepherd (vv. 10–11).

The sum of the poetry is the announcement that Yahweh, God of Israel, is now back in action after a long season of dismay. That new divine action is the emancipation of Jews for homecoming so that they may depart the Babylonian empire and return home to well-being in Jerusalem. We know from elsewhere that this act of emancipation was accomplished by Cyrus the Persian who defeated Babylon and who is termed "Messiah" in the Isaiah poetry (Isa 45:1; see 44:28 as well). It is to be noted that this is the same Cyrus who issued the decree in 2 Chron 36:22–23.

In the gospel narrative it is of course obvious that John, in early Christian reading, is assigned the role of the messenger in Isaiah 40 who will prepare the procession home. While John quotes only these verses in chapter 40, it is clear that his task pertains to the whole of the text of Isaiah concerning *departure* from Babylon and *homecoming* to Jerusalem. In this usage John (and the early church) transposed the poetry in order to apply to a first century crisis of faith. The message is still one of emancipation and homecoming for Jews who had been alienated and marginalized both by Hellenistic culture and Roman governance. The message is still that *departure and homecoming* are to be accomplished by human agency, now Jesus of Nazareth. This is the good news made possible because of Yahweh's empowerment and authorization of emancipatory human agency. John announces nothing less than the end of the power of the old regime and the emergence of a new rule embodied in Jesus.

The New Testament is capable of readily transposing texts into new contexts, drawing the text close to new crisis. John antici-pates that Jesus will enact all of the hopes that Jews held in the first century, in order to recover the freedom and dignity of their Jewishness that had been diminished in a sociopolitical environment that was hostile to Jewishness. The recovery, moreover, is seen as an act of human rehabilitation, with reference to Matthew 11, concerning the many who await restoration and have no hope. Thus an Advent text, placed at the beginning of the gospel narrative, may have been heard by first-century listeners as news about recovered political status, economic possibility, and healthy theological identity. The transposition from Babylon to Rome is an act of imagination that the early church readily makes in its reutilization of Old Testament texts.

Interpretive Imagination

It remains now to consider how the Advent theme *of changed subject,* the character of *John the Baptist* as the last character in the Old Testament, and the quote from *Isaiah 40* about *departure and homecoming* may be heard in contemporary preaching. The decisive themes are still *emancipatory departure and glad homecoming.* It will require, however, a large act of imagination by the preacher to make a connection, for clearly the news is not now heard in the church as departure from Babylon and return to Jerusalem or departure from Roman severity and homecoming to Jewish well-being.

Here is how an act of contemporary interpretive imagination might work. What if, for exile and displacement, we take the alienation and displacement of the contemporary world that turns out to be: a) a mad pursuit of money, success, and security that counts on exaggerated individualism and hostility toward the neighbor, and b) a bewilderment by new technological capacity that leaves the world a strange place or an invitation to hustle harder for more technological leverage. There are a variety of ways in which that alienating environment may be characterized, among them the way of Enlightenment rationality with its passion for control, the intoxicating consumerism that can never be sated, the National Security State that depends on fear and anxiety that commits its citizenry to an endless state of war and therefore an endless fate of amorphous anxiety. However a preacher may characterize it in a local setting (and the preacher has a lot of imaginative alternative ways of lining it out), it is clear that many people who lack labels for it know down deep that our current shared life is in a culture that is, by its very nature, alienating and that causes us to be dissatisfied strangers and restless threats to each other. The truth of that cultural setting is that all of us—liberals and conservatives—are situated in anxiety and endless pursuit of well-being that is always kept out of reach. The situation is not different from that of our ancestors with the *endless brick quotas* of Egypt or the *endless requirements* of "Songs of Zion" in Babylon or the *endless threats* of Rome.

Imagine that the preacher of the gospel has the chance to change the subject: to announce that the fate of Enlightenment reason, frantic consumerism, and the National Security State are not the truth of our lives. The news is that there is a possible departure from the "empire of force" because the empire offeree is not our true home and it could be otherwise.[6] The preacher, in the context of the liturgy, constructs the highway of homecoming that permits us to depart that world that has exerted too much coercive power and that has left us all orphans. The rat race is not where we belong. And we have known since Malachi that reconciling help is on the way. Advent is to start that journey toward our true home given us in the gospel.

Here is the concrete discipline of disengagement and departure offered by John Witte, simply a refusal to play the game and to accept that characterization of our life:

> Both modern technology and modern privacy make escape to the frontier considerably easier than in the days of covered wagons and mule trains. Just turn off Pat Robertson or Jerry Falwell. Turn away the missionary at your door. Close your eyes to the city crucifix that offends. Cover your ears to the public prayer that you can't abide. Forgo the military chaplain's pastoral counseling. Skip the legislative chaplain's prayers. Walk by the town hall's menorah and star. Don't read the Decalogue on the classroom wall. Don't join the religious student group.

6. I take the phrase "empire of force" from Simone Weil; on her usage, see the brilliant exposition of White, *Living Speech: Resisting the Empire of Force*.

Don't vote for the collared candidate. Don't browse the
Evangelicals' newspapers. Avoid the services of the Cath-
olic counselors. Shun the readings of the Scientologists.
Turn down the trinkets of the colporteurs. Turn back
the ministries of the hate-mongers. All these escapes to
the virtual frontier, the law does and will protect—with
force if necessary. Such voluntary self-protections from
religion will ultimately provide far greater religious freedom for all than pressing yet another tired constitutional
case.[7]

But the preacher has more to say than simply the naming of
the lethal system in which we are all variously enmeshed. John's
message, after the hints of Malachi, is not only a critique. It is also
an anticipation. John's work, even as starchy as his critique is, is to
announce the one who is to come. That is the function of his quote
from Isaiah 40. The highway leads somewhere! In the book of Isaiah, the imagined highway *leads to Jerusalem*. In the transposition
of John, of course, it *leads to Jesus*. It leads to the baby who will
confound Herod in Jerusalem. (Remember that on the First Sunday
of Christmas we get Matt 2:13–23 again, the slaughter of the in-
nocents.) It leads to the crucified and risen Lord who will astonish
the authorities in Rome and bewilder the governor. And between
the baby and the crucified one, the road leads to the teacher rabbi
who will astonish by his brave teaching, who will overwhelm by his
inexplicable miracles, who will summon by his authority to a new
life. The path of Advent will lead to Jesus. John belongs to the Old
Testament; Jesus of course belongs to the New Testament, the new
covenant, and the new regime. This is the one through whom "the
blind receive their sight, the lame walk, the lepers are cleansed, the
deaf hear, the dead are raised, and the poor have good news brought
to them" (Matt 11:5).

Advent is to invite people to imagine homecoming. What
would it be like to cross over into the new regime, to come under
the aegis of a new set of commandments and a new set of permis-
sions. All that is required is to desist loyalty to the old order and
take up the new disciplines that entail healing and transforming

7. Witte, *God's Joust, God's Justice*, 262.

and caring. The discipline of Advent is to be ready to entrust life to the coming one.

Such a preached summons will of course evoke explanatory resistance. Every preacher knows about that resistance. And you and I, dear reader, also know the resistance ourselves . . . we have lives to live, we have budgets to raise, we have mortgages to pay, we have obligations to fulfill. Of course! The summons of *Advent departure* and *Christmas homecoming* is not likely to happen by heroic action, though here and there it might. It is more likely to entail steady intentionality that takes a step and a step and a step. I heard a TV preacher on the Exodus; his testimony was that the waters did not part all at once in the Red Sea. When Moses put his foot into the water, it opened a few feet in front of him. Another step and a few more feet of openness, but no opening without a foot in the water. The highway from the empire toward home is like that. It is not an "open road." It appears only enough to take the next step toward home; the road home keeps opening and appearing as we walk the walk.

All that is required in Advent is the recognition that the Old Kingdom of fear, anxiety, and coercion is not our true home. The good news of Advent is that there is another home and there is a path there, the path of intentional Torah obedience that has the neighbor in purview. On Christmas Eve the church makes its defining move from John to Jesus, from old regime to new home. But that moment of break from there to here is not in a vacuum. To get to that wondrous hidden hour of newness, we must be on our way.

The goal of Advent is to come home to Jerusalem, to Jesus, to the neighborhood, to peaceableness where the rule of the God of covenant is under way. At the threshold of home, where the subject has been changed and the road has been walked, the people of the gospel may all echo the well known mantra of the Shaker tradition:

'Tis a gift to be simple, 'tis a gift to be free,
'Tis a gift to come down where we ought to be.

That will preach! 'Tis a gift to be simple after all the *complexities* of the old enslavements that never satisfy. 'Tis a gift to be free after all the old *coercions* that leave us programmed into restless, breathless performance. And it is a gift: "How silently, how silently, the won-drous gift is given!"

In Advent the question is raised: Where ought we to be? Where is our true home? Well, our true home is with Jesus. Our true home is with Jesus' people. Well, our true home is with the lame who now walk, with the lepers who are now healed, with the deaf who now hear, with the dead who now have been raised, with the poor who now have heard good news. That whole company has departed the empire of force and disability in order to spend its time in glad amazement. Think about it! Nobody in Egypt or Babylon or Rome is ever amazed—fatigued, but not amazed. John, with his starchy word, is not the goal of the highway home. But he is the access point. The verse in Isa 40:1, just before the verses quoted by John, affirms that Jerusalem has suffered enough. It is an evangelical word spoken "tenderly" to all the displaced: Enough already! Advent could be among us a sense of self-awareness of the ways in which that old regime has sapped us of our humanness, of our true selves . . . and now we may be welcomed home! But we have to be on our way!

3

Embracing the Transformation
A Comment on Missionary Preaching

> Understanding waits upon conversion, and the primary
> task of the newcomer is a missionary task: to offer a
> persuasive account of a new moral or physical world. He
> must appear to the natives like an eagle at daybreak; they
> have their own owls.[1]

"MISSIONARY PREACHING" IS THE voice of a "newcomer," one who
has something dangerously new to say. "Missionary preaching" intends to make available to the listener the mission—the powerful
mission of God in the world. That mission is an *assertion* (*Gabe*)
of new reality wrought by God, and an *invitation* (*Aufgabe*) to receive and participate in the new reality. In the pulpit at Columbia
Theological Seminary, there is a sign for the eye of the preacher
only. It says, "We would see Jesus."[2] The sign is the urgent request
of the congregation that the preacher focus on making visible the
new evangelical reality at work in the world. Less Christologically

---

1. Walzer, *Interpretation and Social Criticism*, 44. Walzer is speaking ge-
nerically about the missionary task of any missionary and not specifically
about the Christian mission.

2. In a church where I preached recently, the sign for the eyes of the
preacher only said, "Don't Move the Microphone." I could not detect a Christological intention in that expression.

articulated, the sign might say, "Show us the promised land," "Show us the power of God," "'Tell us about the new world," "Announce the news that we may begin again."

Dominant Metaphor

Missionary preaching is simply (to quote Walzer) the "persuasive account of a new world" that is now available because God's purpose, God's intent, God's rule is now in effect. Conversely, the power and claim of all other purposes and all old intentions have been broken. We need no longer live in fear or deference to those old powers or hope for the gifts of those old regimes. The old has passed away; behold, the new has come (2 Cor 5:17).

The central metaphor for this proclamation is the coming of God's governance that displaces, nullifies, and delegitimates every other governance. Martin Buber has seen that the covenant meeting at Sinai was a daring act whereby the rule of Pharaoh was broken by the "Kingship of Yahweh."[3] The same break in power is dramatically asserted in Isaiah 40–55, when the governance of Babylon and of the Babylonian gods is broken by the rule of Yahweh (cf. Isaiah 46–47). In the New Testament, the Markan version of Jesus' self-announcement is a parallel assertion: "The kingdom of God is at hand, repent" (Mark 1:15). The invitations of Moses, Isaiah in exile, and Jesus, the invitation of the whole Bible, is to change the foundational loyalty of our life and to engage in this new loyalty that heals, liberates, and reconciles.[4] The mission of God is to overcome all such deathly powers. Preaching is the invitation to join in that overcoming in order to have life. The central affirmation of every missionary sermon is that the power of deathliness has no more authority or claim over us. We are free for the loyalty appropriate to our life in the world.

---

3. Buber, *The Kingship of God.*

4. After having written this paragraph, I am aware that these three articulations echo the dramatic shaping of the material by Anderson, *The Unfolding Drama of the Bible.*

Thematic Constructs

An amazing fact about the Bible is that the Bible knows that this single, central proclamation must be articulated in a rich, daring variety of ways. It will not do, either in the Bible or in our preaching, simply to reiterate a single formulation of the news, even if we like the sound of that formulation. When we use only a single formulation (or a few variants), the news becomes tired, boring, and reductionist. The challenge of preaching is that this well-known tale of God must be told as if it had never been heard before. The new land must be shown as if it had never been seen before.[5] That fresh telling and that new showing require disciplined, diligent imagination on the part of the preacher.

It is useful, I suggest, to pay attention to some of the central *thematic constructs* of the Bible which shape the assertion (*Gabe*) and the invitation (*Aufgabe*) in different ways. I will mention five such thematic constructs which suggest that the Old Testament text is relentlessly rich and imaginative in articulating the new world of God in which we may live:

1. *Chaos is transformed into creation.* In its largest scope, the Bible invites us to think about God's transformation of the whole cosmos.[6] Much distorted missionary preaching is excessively personalist and privatistic about "me and Jesus." How different if we think of Genesis 1 or Isa 65:17–25 as examples of missionary preaching! These poems assert the news that God has fashioned the chaotic, disordered world into a liveable, ordered home (cf. Isa 45:18–19). We are invited to terminate our complicity in the chaos (either causing chaos or enjoying it), in order to live freely on the terms of the life giving order of God.

Or conversely and even more boldly, the Bible speaks sweepingly about the old creation now hopelessly distorted, so that God works a wholly new recreation. In the new world offered in these texts, old distortions of greed and anxiety are displaced by sharing

---

5. On the prospects for this demanding responsibility, see Craddock, *Overhearing the Gospel*.

6. See Anderson, *Creation versus Chaos*.

and trust. Our preaching is to invite participation in a new creation which is offered as a liveable home.

2. *Despair is overcome by God's promises moving toward fulfillment.* In his magisterial study of the Hexateuch, von Rad has shown how the literature of Genesis–Joshua is organized as the *promise of God* (Gen 12:1–3) moving to the *fulfillment of God* (Josh 21:43–45).[7] The life of Israel is fixed securely between sure promises and trusted fulfillments. Between the promise at the beginning and the fulfillment at the end, there is a buoyancy that knows that this flow of life is being kept, guarded, and guaranteed by God (cf. Hebrews 11). The whole of the Hexateuch is preaching for "missionary work," because these texts present all of life under promise. They invite us to abandon our practice of despair and futility, as though there were no promises and no fulfillments, as though life flatly depended on us. The text asserts we are no longer fated in a world of cosmic indifference, because there is a powerful destiny spoken over us that can be trusted.

3. *This world of harsh injustice is being urged to God's justice.* The story of Israel's monarchy (Samuel and Kings, the pre-exilic prophets) is a story of fearful self-serving power which is brutal and selfish. We find ourselves not far removed from such power which works deep injustice and which seems set to last forever. But the text, through the voice of the prophets, gives account of another purpose, a purpose of care, compassion, and fidelity, which relentlessly protests against the brutality and finally has its way.[8] This alternative account of Israel's life (told, for example, through the tale of Naboth's vineyard, or Hezekiah's prayer, or Amos's judgment, or Jeremiah's tears) asserts that Israel's life is not a flat, closed history. Israel's life is a demanding choice between two ways, one of which leads to life and one of which leads to death (cf. Deut 30:15–20). In the context of the kings of Israel and Judah, this entire literature of kings and prophets is an exposé of injustice and an assertion that the rule of God's caring justice finally is the wave of the future. This sad story of the monarchy and the determined poetry of the

---

7. Von Rad, "The Problem of the Hexateuch."
8. See Brueggemann, *Prophetic Imagination.*

prophets, together are a summons to leave off old ways of manipulation and control in order to embrace the possibility of communal justice appropriate to God's new rule.

4. *In a world of exile, there is a powerful impetus to come home.* The literature of the exile is a statement acknowledging what it is like to be displaced, alienated, and abandoned.[9] This earlier literature draws very close to the alienation of modern life. "Exile" is a pertinent metaphor for much of our present experience. The literature, however, does not dwell on the reality of exile, nor on the route into exile. It focuses rather on going home, on being cared for and led home by a God who fights for us like a warrior (Is. 40:10) and who carries us gently like a mother (Isa 40:11; 49:14–16).

5. *The wisdom of God is overcoming the foolishness of the world.*[10] The wisdom tradition of Proverbs and Job seems an unlikely locus for missional preaching. Yet even these texts bear witness to a different world where God governs.[11] The book of Proverbs is about the world of foolishness which brings death, a foolishness based in greed, selfishness, indifference, and the yearning for a "quick fix." The new world of God, offered as an alternative by the wisdom teachers, is one wisely ordered that yields life and well-being to those who are obediently discerning. The poem of Job, in a quite different idiom, reflects on the killing, isolated outcome of a life lived in stultifying conformity (Job's friends) or in arrogant defiance (Job). The book of Job invites us to a different world in which the wonder of God is visible and acknowledged (Job 38:1—41:34), and in which the terrible options of conformity and defiance are overcome (42:1–6).

These five categories are enormously suggestive and comprehend in a general way much of the text of the Old Testament.

1. *Chaos* becoming *creation* or new creation (Genesis 1–11)

2. *Despair* yielding to *promise* toward fulfillment
(Genesis–Joshua)

---

9. See Klein, *Israel in Exile.*

10. This formulation is, of course, an inversion of 1 Cor 1:18–25. The inversion is required because, in the end, it is God's foolishness which is wise.

11. See von Rad, *Wisdom in Israel.*

3. *Injustice* overridden by God's *justice* (Samuel, Kings, Prophets)

4. *Exiles* invited *home* (exilic literature)

5. *Foolishness* overcome by *wisdom* (Proverbs, Job)

This is not an exhaustive list of the theological-literary thematic constructs available in Old Testament literature, which are ways to present the new rule of God.[12] It is, however, a sufficient sample from which to observe the various ways in which the Old Testament lends itself to missional preaching. These theological-literary constructs are not yet the concrete stuff of preaching. They are only general models in which the texts are located, and they provide for us general interpretive clues. Three observations occur to me about this inventory.

First, there is *rich variety* in these constructs. No one of these thematics is more basic than another, though we may each have our favorite. Each makes its own peculiar statement and must be taken on its own terms. None should be flattened or reduced to sound like any others.

Second, each in its own way concerns the *transformative enterprise* of God that is under way, in which we are invited to participate.

- Chaos is *being transformed* into creation.

- Despair is *being transformed* into fulfilled promises.

- Injustice is *being transformed* into a community of justice.

- Exile is *being transformed* into homecoming.

- Foolishness that kills is *being transformed* into wisdom which gives life.

In each case, the world is no longer what it was. The world is not as we thought it was, or as it appeared to be. A new world is, in the moment of the text (and our speech about the text), being offered and made available.

12. Among the other thematic constructs which might be discussed are: a) the move from lament to praise in the Psalms; b) tales of inversion in the books of Genesis, Numbers, and Kings; and c) apocalyptic anticipations in Zechariah and Daniel.

Third, these several thematic constructs are not flat descriptions or reports. They are rather *powerful appeals for us to discern the world differently,* to discern the world afresh, to receive a quite fresh perspective on the world through these particular articulations. The texts are not neutral observations, but they are powerful arguments that because of God's gospel, the world we live in is not the one we have been led to embrace.

The Specificity of the Text

We have moved in our analysis from *dominant metaphor* to *thematic constructs.* Now we make a second move toward greater specificity. What is preached is not a slogan about the new kingdom. What is preached is not a set of formal constructs. What is to be preached is the *specificity of the text* in order to permit *a weaned imagination.*

Three Examples

I assume that every missional sermon is the explication of a specific text as a peculiar presentation of a changed governance. I will suggest three examples of how we might move from *dominant metaphor* to *thematic construct* to *specific text.*

   1. *Micah 4:1–4*
      a) The dominant metaphor: *God's new rule*
      b) The thematic construct: *chaos became creation*
      c) The specific text

> . . . they shall beat their swords into plowshares,
>   and their spears into pruning hooks;
> nation shall not lift up sword against nation,
>   neither shall they learn war any more;
> but they shall sit every man
>   under his vine and under his fig tree,
>   and none shall make them afraid . . . (Mic 4:3–4).[13]

13. The entire poetic unit of vv. 1–4 (5) must, of course, be treated. Because of space limitations, I have quoted only a portion of the unit.

We live in a world of chaos. Nobody needs more evidence for that. It is a world of greedy insecurity in which we want more and more fig trees and vines. We never seem to have enough to be satisfied. The reason we are driven by such greedy insecurity is that we have chosen to live by sword and spear, by weapons of aggression, intimidation, and brutality. The combination of greedy insecurity and weapons of brutality, of course, yields a world of chaos. They leave us very much afraid. The world is nonetheless being transformed. Creation is being made new. It is being made new in the very moment of this text. While we listen to the poem, we notice that fewer vines and fig trees might satisfy us, if only we begin to refashion our swords and spears into gardening tools to care for the earth and let it produce. The very poem and the sermon we preach are a part of the scenario of transformation. By the end of the poem, by the conclusion of the sermon, our weapons are slightly reshaped. We have had a slight move towards disarmament, not only in the big "Cold War," but in all the "cold wars" we fight every day. We find our chaos is a bit tamed. We have a glimpse of what it is like with God's new rule. We have a new hope and yearning that we could live, at home and everywhere, with "none to make afraid." We have now heard the invitation grounded in God's action.

2. *Exodus 15:20–21*
   a) The dominant metaphor: *God's new rule*
   b) The thematic construct: *despair transformed*
        by God's promise
   c) The specific text

> Then Miriam, the prophetess, the sister of Aaron, took a timbrel in her hand; and all the women went out after her with timbrels and dancing. And Miriam sang to them: "Sing to Yahweh, for he has triumphed gloriously; the horse and his rider he has thrown into the sea." (Exod 15:20–21)

We live, like ancient Israel, in a world of slavery, unreasonable expectations, and hopeless quotas. We are pursued by peer pressure, debts to be paid, social expectation, the daily drive for food. We endlessly produce and it is never enough. That world of pressured production is deeply without hope, a dead place without promise. At the edge of that dead place, however, if we listen carefully, we can hear a new, faint piece of music that, while we listen, grows louder and more compelling. The music has an odd beat, the sound of liberated tambourines. We rush to the edge of the empire from where the sound is coming. When we arrive at the edge (where we never dared go before), we find our sister Miriam and many other sisters dancing and singing with abandonment. Their bodies look exhausted from the accumulation of too much work and too much hopelessness. But the tambourines summon their feet, and they cannot keep still, tired as they are. We watch their dance. Now they are not tired because they are not in despair. They have slipped over the border of the empire and stand outside it. We listen to the song, and in the singing we hear the name of this God, Yahweh, who is strong and powerful, who has drowned the horses, killed the warriors, ridden the sea—all the way to freedom.

We listen cynically to the song, because we are modern. We do not believe in silly miracles, because Pharaoh is forever. There are, moreover, no promises that the corporation has not co-opted. At least there is none known to us. Even in our cynicism, however, there is something haunting about the tambourine. Even more haunting is the look of rest and joy in the tired faces of the women, the sense of well-being and starting again that we never expected. The tambourine does not lie. Even if the song is primitive, it is transformative. We begin a cautious foot-tapping and soon we have tentatively joined the song of freedom. The God who made the old promises has acted. The production quotas will no longer control our life—we sing all the way to freedom, and we will not again knuckle under to the quota and the pressure. It is strange, but the very song of Miriam (and the sermon we hear about the dancing) is itself the very process of transformation and liberation. The song sets us a little free and we will never fully regress again. We have been at the edge of the empire, and we have looked outside the empire to the dance. We notice what it is like when we shake off the weight of despair.

3. *Proverbs 15:17*
    a) The dominant metaphor: *God's new rule*
    b) The thematic construct: *wisdom overpowering foolishness*
    c) The concrete text

> Better is a dinner of herbs where love is
> than a fatted ox and hatred with it. (Prov 15:17)

What we eat shapes our life. We have to watch what we eat. There are so many ways to be stupid about food. There are too many kinds of junk food, some cheap and greasy, some highly caloric, some exotic and costly. The more affluent we become, the more we imagine that every meal should be a rich feast. The more affluent we become, the more intense the social whirl, inviting and being invited, fed to exhaustion. We have to keep up appearances and return obligations. "We are going out and the sitter will fix pot pies for the children." The whirl leaves us exhausted. It is almost no fun anymore. But we cannot offend this fast style. "If we don't keep it up, we will be dropped, and anyway, the kids like the sitter better than us." One way is fatted ox, seafood, prime beef, with exhaustion and alienation. Another way is to simplify, disengage, get healthy, and slow down—eat greens, herbs, spinach. The alternative is not to "graze" but to eat, surrounded by a family with stories to tell and jokes to enjoy, laughs to share, hurts to pool, fears to embrace— "where love is." When a semblance of order returns to our consuming, the meal feels like the kingdom of God. The new rule has overwhelmed our hastened, desperate affluence concerning junk food and junk life. So we sing, "Forgive our foolish ways, Reclothe us in our rightful minds" with sane eating and caring.

The text is such a simple proverb. The patient, gentle discernment of what is "better," nevertheless, lets us leave off the killing foolishness. The proverb is unpacked at the dining room table in the presence of the whole family. The proverb transforms our foolish, deathly life into a feast of the kingdom—greens!

These three texts are so very different—Micah hoping, Miriam dancing, and Solomon advising. Each text bears a witness: Micah from *chaos to creation*, Miriam *from despair to promise*, Solomon *from foolishness to wisdom*. All three texts bear witness to the new rule of God, the new rule present in the text itself, a new world given in the act of our listening. In each rendering of the text, the preacher must attend to:

- the central claim of a new governance;
- the thematic construct that shapes the transformation;
- the detail of image and the nuance of the text.

A Weaned Imagination

The purpose of a textual, missional sermon is to help listeners participate in the transformation God is now working, working in the process of the text and its proclamation. That is, the purpose of such a sermon is to let us be transformed. The sermon is not to talk about a transformation that happens somewhere else with someone else at another time. It is a transformation that happens now with us, here, in this moment of speaking and hearing (cf. Deut 5:3). We need to ask: How do people like us change? How does transformation happen? While we do not know fully, this much seems clear. Serious preaching that evokes change aims not at doctrinal clarification or moral rectitude (either conservative or liberal), but at a weaned, newly-authorized imagination.

By "imagination" I mean the pictures, images, and metaphors we have in our heads that shape our world and determine our actions and values.[14] These images are elemental and preconceptual, having been acquired in prerational kinds of ways. They are not changed by rational argument. They are changed by being displaced by a more compelling set of images and narratives that have authority in our most elemental experiences.

When we belong to the old world—of chaos, despair, injustice, exile, and foolishness—we act out that world. If the world is perceived and experienced as chaos, we will act chaotically. We have been a long time learning to trust in and rely upon those *un*-evangelical images of the world. "Missionary preaching" seeks to offer a more compelling set of images rooted in our deepest tradition and

14. See Coulson, *Religion and Imagination*.

making contact with our memory and hope. Such preaching seeks eventually to wean our imagination away from the deathliness of a world where God does not govern.

Thus, for example, Micah's contemporaries lived in an imagined world of swords, spears, and greedy scarcity. Micah *imagined* with them a different world, a world of disarmament and contentment and security. He invited his listeners to live toward that alternative world. Miriam's contemporaries *imagined* a hopeless world of Pharaoh's brick quotas. Miriam and her sisters danced an alternative of promise and possibility, outside the scope of the empire. Solomon's greedy people *imagined* a world of junk food and junk living. The wisdom teacher *imagined* a "better" world. In each of these three cases, the new world offered is only an act of imagination, not more.

- The world of swords and spears still exists after Micah's poem, but we imagine pruning hooks and plowshares.

- The world of Pharaoh and bricks still exists after Miriam's dance, but we imagine tambourines, dancing, and freedom.

- The world of junk food is still seductive after Solomon's proverb, but we imagine a family happily gathered around spinach.

Little by little, our imagination can be weaned away from false "world proposals" that are the ideology and propaganda of the "rulers of this age." When our imagination is weaned away from falseness and death, the new rule of God has a chance. We imagine plowshares, tambourines, and spinach. We hope differently on that basis, care differently, dance differently, eat differently—in a very different world, a world given us by the text.

Relinquish and Embrace

The text of course seems remote from our daily experience. It is the important, demanding task of the preacher to let the text touch in authoritative ways the concreteness of our imagination. The main claims of missional preaching, as I have suggested them, are:

Embracing the Transformation

- We live in a situation (world) that needs transformation.
- The news is that the decisive transformation has happened. (All of these texts witness to that conviction.)
- We can participate in the unfinished business of the transformation—

  by following the transformation wrought through the text;

  by yielding our deathly images to be available for new images given us in the gospel and its poetry;

  by acting on the basis of the new claims of creation / promise / justice / homecoming / wisdom.

The interpretive problem is this: How do I discern and experience this new reality given in the text? Missional preaching not only makes an assertion. It issues an invitation. The invitation is to *relinquish* the old world of death, to *embrace* the new world of life. The drama of relinquishing and embracing is the crucial, ongoing, unfinished drama of our life. For each of us, the invitation entails different actions and different transformation. But there is also a commonality about our situation. I suggest that in the United States, in the next years of our preaching, the *relinquishment* to which we are summoned is to break free of the *ideology of consumerism* that dominates our culture and the allied *deception of militarism* that keeps us in bondage. Such a relinquishment is a tall order indeed, perhaps one about which we have no agreement. What we probe for is the concrete experience in our life of the power of chaos/despair/injustice/exile/foolishness. I submit that the worldview of consumer militarism (or conversely militaristic consumerism) touches every aspect of our life, engendering despair, fear, greed, and finally brutality among us.

Missional preaching is to make evident the deathliness of our present idolatry and to present the good news of another counter-reality. This deathly power that besets us—

- touches *public policy,* in terms of defense, welfare, taxation, and even our view of capital punishment;

- touches *interpersonal relations* so that persons in marriage and family relations and in other face-to-face relations are treated as useable commodities, or as conforming automatons;

- touches *personal self-concepts* fostering a sense either of needing to be a consumer or a producer, ready to be hedonistic or useful, in either case debased from personhood and therefore increasingly numbed;

- touches our *perception of the world* as a cosmic orphanage where we live continually under enormous threat;

- touches our *view of God* who is variously an awesome judge who punishes wrongdoing or a doting friend who is utterly tolerant.

Such an ideological view—chaotic as Micah's world, enslaving as Miriam's world, brutalizing as Solomon's foolish eaters—will destroy us.

The news to be proclaimed in missional preaching is that an alternative world is possible and offered because a faithful God rules.

- *Public Policy* can be compassionate and caring when free of the deathliness of militarism.

- *Other persons* can be friends and neighbors when not pressured by utility.

- *The self* can be celebrated as a beloved, summoned heir of God when we are freed of consumptive, productive models of self.

- *The world* can be appreciated as a network of life-giving forces when exploitation of creation is stopped.

- *God* can be recognized as a faithful, generous, demanding partner when our distortions of works righteousness and cheap grace are relinquished.

Every and any person can join the mission and share in the transformation. Any and every person can make important moves towards the new governance. We are invited into the transformation by "the renewal of our minds" (Rom 12:2). The new governance, however, requires that we not be "conformed." Preaching is an imaginative empowerment for transformation when our minds, hearts, and imagination are reinstructed.

Settled but Unfinished Transformation

The massive possibility in such preaching is that the world will be re-perceived and re-engaged as God's creation, now being freshly renewed. It is this settled but unfinished transformation that must be preached. In such preaching we assert:

1. *The truth of the transformation.* Missional preaching must affirm in as many modes and ways as possible that a new world of creation, promise, justice, homecoming, and wisdom has indeed begun.

2. *The hiddenness of the transformation.* It belongs to God's way that the new world comes like "a thief in the night," noticed only by those who watch for its coming. The loud, shrill power of the old world still fascinates us. We must be attentive to the alternative if we are to notice.

3. *The demand of the transformation.* The deep gift of God is free, but it is costly. No one enters this new world easily, casually, or accidentally. Entry requires an intentional embrace, and a knowing relinquishment.

4. *The polemic of the transformation.* This preaching and the choices it requires are not "tolerant" or "evenhanded." The gospel is no friend of Pharaoh or death. The enemy is concretely named, and we must be prepared to name the deathliness that is operative in public policy, in our personal, intimate lives, and everywhere that we seek a newness.

5. *The joy and freedom of the transformation.* The assertion and invitation of missional preaching is an offer that we can now, as never before, become who we are meant to be, at peace, in joy, safe, cared for, empowered. This joy

contrasts deeply and decisively with the failure of the living death all around us.

We began with a wondrous quote from Walzer. There really is "a new world." That new world requires a "persuasive account." That new world requires that the preacher be "like an eagle at daybreak"—fresh, awesome, daring, sure, and powerful. Too much of our preaching is like an owl at dusk—settled, wise, and dull; or like a pigeon at midnight—tired, unimpressive, fearful, sapped of energy. The transformation mediated in this text is for the congregation. It is, however, also for the preacher, that the preacher should be transformed from owl or pigeon to eagle. The text and the gospel intend that the preacher is one who may mount up on wings like an eagle, in order that the rest of us should

> run and not be weary,
>> walk and not faint. (Isa 40:31)

When the eagle comes with a new world,

> we shall dream with Micah,

>> we shall dance with Miriam,

>>> we shall eat herbs with love.

The new world, birthed in the sermon—which permits new dreaming, new dancing, new eating—evokes new, joyous living. We are then no longer conformed, but utterly transformed. We have our minds renewed, our lives changed, and our world begins again.

4

From Windows Overlooking the Street

I HAVE BEEN PONDERING words from Woodrow Wilson, son of Davidson College, that he wrote while still an academic. He wrote them in 1891 in *The Atlantic Monthly*, words reprinted in a more recent issue of that journal. Wilson considers what it is that causes some books to become "immortal," long-lasting in influence and stature. And then Wilson wonders about the kinds of authors who can produce such books. As an author who is well short of any book that is "immortal," I find his words nonetheless instructive to me:

> It is best for the author to be born away from literary centres, or to be excluded from their ruling set if he be born in them. It is best that he start out with his thinking, not knowing how much has been thought and said about everything. A certain amount of ignorance will insure his sincerity, will increase his boldness and shelter his genuineness, which is his hope of power. Not ignorance of life, but life may be learned in any neighborhood;—not ignorance of the greater laws which govern human affairs, but they may be learned without a library of historians and commentators, by imaginative sense, by seeing better than by reading;—not ignorance of the infinitudes of human circumstance, but knowledge of these may come to a man without the intervention of universities;—not ignorance of one's self and of one's

neighbor, but innocence of the sophistications of learning, its research without love, its knowledge without inspiration, its method without grace; freedom from its shame at trying to know many things as well as from its pride of trying to know but one thing.[1]

These words are important to me because they resonate well with the "ignorance" entrusted to me by my disadvantaged educational history. And then Wilson writes words that for me have a much broader significance:

> The ability to see for one's self is attainable, not by mixing with crowds and ascertaining how they look at things, but by a certain aloofness and self-containment. The solitariness of some genius is not accidental; it is characteristic and essential. To the constructive imagination there are some immortal feats which are possible only in seclusion. The man must heed first and most of all the suggestions of his own spirit; and the world can be seen from windows overlooking the street better than from the street itself.[2]

The mark of writing that has a chance of durable import, he suggests, is the consequence of a closely guarded and relished privacy for those who are not too busy networking too widely or intensely, but who make room for brooding and independent thought of a courageous kind.

Of course the readership of the *Journal of Preachers* is not committed primarily to the writing of books, immortal or otherwise. But it strikes me that Wilson's wise words may, beyond the production of books, be worth considering in two other zones.

First, it occurs to me that these words may be good counsel to pastors. There is no doubt that pastors need to be in touch with folks, to network and be attentive with all due grace to social interaction and expectation. But the church—and even more the society around the church—does not need winsome or skilled social directors. Given the power of an anti-life ideology in our society and

---

1. Wilson, "How Books Become Immortal," 58–60.
2. Ibid., 60.

given the temptation of the church to dumb down, the church urgently needs pastors who are thoughtful, informed, well-grounded, and alert to the connections that lie well beneath the surface. Most especially in the Reformed tradition but more generally in all old-line churches, there is an urgent need to *think* the faith. And that cannot be done by e-mail messages or the last news summary or the latest press conference or fad. There is of course great merit in being "on the street itself." But there are limits to what can come from such engagement that stays on the surface. Beyond that, pastors will have a fresh word and a good word from time spent with the classics of the theological tradition and with enough free time to ponder connections and interfaces that one may receive from "the windows overlooking the street." Wilson's words suggest to me a recovery of the critical intellectual task of the church, for somebody among us now needs to *think* in a society where thinking has all but disappeared.

Second, as a theological educator, I wonder about seminarians, college students, and other young people who strike this old guy as excessively "connected." (And from that I wonder about "youth ministry" that tends to border on entertainment. We seem to forget in much of that process that we are nurturing the next wave of disciples who can stand before the authorities with the truth given us.) There is no doubt that e-mail can savage one's time and yield the illusion that one is at work or even being educated. There is no doubt, moreover, that excessive cell phone contact extends adolescence and slows the hard process of becoming free, "autonomous" moral and intellectual agents. Of course the old model of isolated learners is not one to which any of us would return. But there is a place in nurture and education for independence, risk, responsibility, and accountability. One may wonder where the leadership will come from in time to come, with enough sustained, grounded self to step out front without checking first to see that everyone else is also headed there.

I assume Wilson would not have written these words back then unless he sensed a problem with excessive connectedness. How much more now! The outcome of such connectedness may be humaneness and a gentle attentiveness; but such acute interdependence also leads to an *ersatz* therapeutic propensity that does not specialize in moral courage or daring thought. There is no doubt that Jesus regularly withdrew from the crowds, "the street," to pray. It must also have been the case that he withdrew to ponder the tradition in which he stood and its promises, and to reread his context from the angle of that tradition. Prayer and thought go together but should not be confused with each other. They both require moral courage that will not be nourished by too much "group think." The process of individuation matters among those who might, on some occasion, be able to say with freedom, "Thus saith the Lord."

5

Ministry Among

The Power of Blessing

THE NOTION OF "NORTH America as a mission field" is a breath-taking idea after we have for so long thought we "took" the gospel to the "benighted" elsewhere. Now we are talking about a mission to those close at hand, those near to us, those among us who are most like us. This little essay considers one biblical resource for such a shift of perspective, a shift that among other things perhaps entails a refocus in the Bible itself.

The Gospel Beforehand

In his argument for the gospel among the Gentiles, Paul writes:

> And the scripture, foreseeing that God would justify the Gentiles by faith, declared *the gospel beforehand* to Abraham, saying, "All the Gentiles shall be blessed in you." For this reason, those who believe are blessed with Abraham who believed. (Gal 3:8–9)

Paul here quotes Gen 12:3b, part of God's initial mandate to Abraham. Oddly, Paul terms this formulation "the gospel beforehand," (*proeuangellion*), the good news of God's governance that has been known and uttered in Israel from the outset. What Paul knows is that the gospel, from the outset, has been concerned for a defining and transformative relationship between *the called community of Yahweh* and *all the others* among whom the faithful live. The formulation of Gen 12:3/Gal 3:8 focuses upon "be blessed." I propose that our rethinking of "mission among" may be understood as a mission of blessing, a way of speaking and thinking and acting that is very different from our usual missional rhetoric.

We may understand God's final promise to Abraham in 12:3 as the culmination of a "theory of Israel" that shapes the book of Genesis and the entire Torah:[1]

1.   Blessing theology is creation theology.[2] That is, the creation texts of the Old Testament affirm that God has blessed, ordained fruitfulness and well-being, bestowed on the processes of creation the capacity for well-being and fulfillment of its true destiny of abundance: "God blessed them, saying, 'Be fruitful and multiply and fill the waters in the seas, and let birds multiply on the earth'" (Gen 1:22).[3] The "force for life" has been implanted by the creator into all of creation. It is this "force for life" that constitutes the substance of blessing.

2.   On its own terms and without any dogmatic imposition of a notion of "the fall," the Genesis account of the world indicates that the defining blessing of God for the world has

1. Von Rad, "The Form-critical Problem of the Hexateuch." On the linkage of Genesis 1–11 and the ancestral narratives, von Rad writes: "Thus the opening words of the story of redemption provide the answer to the problem posed by the early history of the world, that of the relationship of God to the nations as whole. The beginning of the story of redemption in Gen. XII.1–3, however, not only brings to an end the early history, as Budde rightly saw, but actually provides the key to it," 65. Von Rad's insight has been elaborated by many scholars.

2. The most helpful and accessible study of blessing is by Westermann, *Blessing in the Bible and the Life of the Church.* See also his little book, *Creation.*

3. The derivative blessing of humanity is in 1:28; that blessing is clearly subordinate as the man and the woman are a subset of creation. Attention should be paid to Exod 1:7. In that text it is Israel who "multiplies," thus embodying the blessings meant for creation. On the reiteration of the terms, see Brueggemann, "The Kerygma of the Priestly Writers."

been resisted and distorted (perhaps nullified?) by the recalcitrance of the creation. As Gerhard von Rad and many others have seen, the sequence of narratives about Adam and Eve (Genesis 2–3), Cain and Abel (Genesis 4), the flood (Genesis 6–9), and the Tower of Babel (Gen 11:1–9) constitutes an inventory of the recalcitrance and resistance that marks the world of the nations.[4] The outcome of these narratives is that the blessing of God for creation has been thwarted; the world is now defined by curse . . . perhaps curse as the direct assertion of divine threat or perhaps simply as an outcropping of consequences of choices without any divine intrusion.[5] Either way, the "force for life" generously given by Yahweh is ineffective and the world is beset by *alienation, anxiety,* and *brutality.*[6]

3. And then, abruptly, comes "the gospel beforehand" to father Abraham and the communities derivative from Abraham (Jews, Christians, Muslims). "The families of the earth" to whom Abraham is to be a blessing, as Hans Walter Wolff has seen, are all those in Genesis 3–11 who have dropped out of the power of Yahweh's blessing, who by dropping out "became futile in their thinking and their senseless minds were darkened" (Rom 1:21; see 8:20; Eph 4:17).[7] As the story stands, however, the "families of the earth" are more specifically and concretely those other ethnic, social, and territorial communities with whom the ancestors—Abraham and his family—must deal on a daily basis. That is, the reference to the nations has a twofold reference, one more intensely theological, the other

---

4. See von Rad, *Old Testament Theology*, vol. 1, 154–60.

5. Koch has argued powerfully for *consequences* rather than divine intrusion ("Is There a Doctrine of Retribution in the Old Testament?").

6. See below on these terms. My intent is to specify the meaning of "curse" that is reflected in Gen 3:14, 17; 4:11; 9:25; and differently 8:21. The terms I have used here suggest what I take to be contemporary dimensions of the power of the curse.

7. Wolff, "The Kerygma of the Yahwist." Much of my argument here is derivative from Wolff.

quite practical as "living among" without all of the dark theological rhetoric that is familiar to us from Paul. In this latter sense, the "families of the earth" are not some symbolic cipher to serve theology, but they are real people who dispute with Israel about land, water rights, and all the inevitable disputes of social existence.

The formula of Gen 12:3, "the gospel beforehand," occurs as a fixed formula five times in the ancestral narratives, clearly a quite intentional, programmatic utterance that gives shape to the disparate narratives.

In Gen 12:3, the formula is given no specificity. Except that in 12:6 we are told, "at that time the Canaanites were in the land" (see 13:7). Of course, that is why it is called "land of Canaan" (12:5–6). Whether he likes it or not, Abraham is placed among Canaanites by the God who makes promises.[8]

The formula is repeated to Abraham in Gen 18:18. The verse is followed by the odd phrasing of v. 19: "I have chosen him, that he may charge his children and his household after him to keep the way of the Lord by doing righteousness and justice; so that the Lord may bring about for Abraham what he has promised him." This remarkable verse is the only usage in Genesis of the Mosaic-prophetic word pair "justice and righteousness." The couplet imports into the ancestral narrative the large social vision of Israel at its prophetic best. The nations are "blessed" when the people of Abraham practice righteousness and justice, that is, when they order social power in community-generating ways.

The third articulation to Abraham (Gen 22:18, at the end of the narrative of sacrifice) suggests that Abraham's way with the "nations" is one of radical obedience to God that entails deep, costly, risky sacrifice. The odd calculus of this paragraph is that Abraham, in obedience to God, risks all; the result is that the force

8. The term "Canaanite" undoubtedly is not an ethnic term. It is rather a sociological, ideological term. Thus the Canaanites and the Israelites who polemize against the Canaanites are in every respect exactly alike, except the theological, ideological loyalties that distinguish them. The Canaanites are "neighbors" who are close at hand, but who confess different loyalties and so organize socio-economic, political power differently.

of generative creation (blessing) is offered for all the others. (The ecclesial implication is one of deep discipline.)

The declaration of "the gospel beforehand" to Isaac in Gen 26:4–5 reiterates the claim of obedience in 22:18. Again it is the radical obedience of Abraham that counts for the nations. It is noteworthy that the promise made to Isaac appeals yet again to the obedience of his father, thus making unmistakable that the ministry of blessing" is intergenerational. That is, the blessing of Abraham for the nations is extended "into the third and fourth generations." Isaac is invited to share in the alternative world of blessing, even though he is given no direct command to obey.

The reiteration of the formula to Jacob (Gen 28:14) is in the context of many other, more personal promises to Jacob. While the formulation itself adds nothing new, in the narrative that follows even the cunning Laban can deduce that Jacob is a source of blessing in his life: "If you will allow me to say so, I have learned by divination that Yahweh has blessed me because of you" (Gen 30:27).

These five formulations are a quite intentional theological shaping of the ancestral narrative. These ancestors are presented— and inside the narrative understand themselves—as a center of blessing, a concentrated locus of the "life force" of Yahweh in the world.

Blessing and New Life

It is important that we should be clear about this matter of blessing, for it is not a common point in our theology, leave alone in our notion of mission. Blessing is first to be understood in these narratives as a *material* process of new life that is *intrinsic* to creation that arises when the generative powers of creation function as God has intended and decreed them. It is important that in the notion of blessing, the emblem of the *generative powers of creation* is in the birth of children, more specifically in a patriarchal society, the birth of sons. Thus the ancestral narratives are endlessly preoccupied with the question of arrival of the next generation, and as we have seen, in the Jacob narrative even the production of valuable animals. The blessing arises in the midst of the processes of daily life when all works well. This same celebration of generativity (expressed in quite male language) is voiced in the Psalms:

> Sons are indeed a heritage from Yahweh,
> > the fruit of the womb a reward.
> Like arrows in the hand of a warrior
> > are the sons of one's youth.
> Happy is the man who has
> > his quiver full of them.
> He shall not be put to shame
> > when he speaks with his enemies in the gate. (Ps 127:3–5)

> Happy is everyone who fears Yahweh,
> > who walks in his ways . . .
> Your wife will be like a fruitful vine within your house;
> > your children will be like olive shoots around your table.
> Thus shall the man be blessed
> > who fears Yahweh.
> Yahweh bless you from Zion.
> > May you see the prosperity of Jerusalem
> > all the days of your life.
> May you see your children's children.
> > Peace be upon Israel. (Ps 128:1, 3–6)[9]

9. Psalm 128 uses two different terms for "blessing." The term "happy" speaks of a more material, secular notion of blessing, whereas "blessed" in the latter verse is a more theological term. The two, however, are used together, thus bringing close together the practical matter of material prosperity and the acknowledgement of Yahweh as the God who blesses with prosperity. For an analysis of this formulation, see Hanson, "How Honorable! How Shameful."

I should acknowledge that the valuing of children (sons) in the contemporary world is not directly and fully taken over from that ancient world, given the industrial revolution and the lesser economic need for children. While acknowledging that fact, one may still notice: a) in a nursing home the presence of a baby to touch and smell is indeed taken as a foundational sign of hope; b) given all we know about birthing processes, it is still noteworthy that many couples desiring children go to great lengths, medically and economically, to secure children. The issues are not the same as in the ancient world. But they are not, in many cases, very different. A child is still in many ways the quintessential gift of the creator.

The second facet of blessing important to understand is this: while blessing as life-force that produces generative, productive, material prosperity is intrinsic to life-processes themselves, blessing can be *bestowed, transferred from* one party to another in an almost palpable way. Here we move into a mystery of life that does not admit of scientific or technical explanation. We are closer to a sacramental dimension of reality, whereby those who possess God's life-force in abundance can share and distribute it among others who may be deficient in what is needed for life.

We can readily identify two primary centers for the power of blessing:

1. The family is the primal matrix of blessing that stretches intergenerationally. In Genesis 49, the old man Jacob still is master of the life-force as he had been when he was a blessing to Laban. Indeed, all through the narrative, Jacob drips with the power to enhance life. In chapter 49, the old man assembles his sons; he speaks a blessing over each of them, empowering them to appropriate the future that is peculiarly theirs: "All these are the twelve tribes of Israel, and this is what their father said to them when he blessed them, blessing each one of them with a suitable blessing" (v. 28; see also Deuteronomy 33).

More contentiously and with less equanimity, this same Jacob, though younger, is a the key player in Genesis 27 where the brothers dispute the blessing. Jacob "steals" the blessing from Esau to whom it rightly belongs. Deceived Isaac blesses deceiving Jacob, giving him access to power for the future (27:27–29; note that the last phrasing of v. 29 echoes the words addressed to Abraham in Gen 12:3). By the time Isaac finishes speaking, the blessing is assigned. It has been transmitted and cannot be recalled. This in turn produces the pathos of Esau: "'Bless me, me also father!' . . . 'Have you not reserved a blessing for me? . . . Have you only one blessing, father? Bless me, me also, father!' And Esau lifted up his voice and wept" (vv. 34–38).

Families are arenas for blessing (and curse). Parents do bestow blessing on children (and withhold), by gesture, word, touch, and in all kinds of subtle, less direct ways. Every family has a member(s) who is more powerful and who can generate futures for others. And most every family has people who are left out, like Esau.

2. A second arena of blessing is the priestly function when the power of blessing is known to be concentrated in a sacred place.[10] Indeed, people come there precisely for a blessing, to have transmitted to them in sacral ways the power for life to choose a future. The best known example, still echoed by us, is the priestly blessing of Num 6:24–26, whereby Aaron and his sons bestow upon Israel a future of grace and peace. (It is too bad, in my judgment, that in much of the church the priestly authority to bless has been trivialized, likely because the priests themselves are embarrassed by such power or do not believe in it, and so the benediction becomes, all too often, nothing more than a signing off with "good luck.")

The ancestral narrative, playing upon the claims of *family* and *priests*, makes the claim that the power of blessing is concentrated in this community of faith. That power of blessing concentrated in Israel is no property for Israel. It is "by you" that the power of blessing shall be transmitted to and for the others who have, since their embrace of curse, been deficient in the power to choose a prosperous future.

A Viable Future of Shalom

Insofar as this line of interpretation is useful, it needs to be understood that I am urging a quite different notion of "ministry among." It is to be observed that Abraham and his kin never directly confront the nations with their faith, never seek to recruit or convert. Rather the power of blessing is a free gift offered to the nations, as its has been a free entrustment to Israel. The purpose of blessing is not to enhance Israel nor even, we may believe, to accent the importance of Yahweh. It is rather that the community should "work," as more and more people are included in the power of blessing and so freed of the dread, deathly force of curse. I do not imagine that this is all that can be said about "ministry among," but it is an important

---

10. See Westermann, "Creation and History in the Old Testament"; and Westermann, *What Does the Old Testament Say about God?*

motif that may stop well short of a desperate triumphalism that understands mission as imposition.

Thus I propose that "ministry among" consists, as it did for the ancestors, in being visibly available with the life-force of a viable future of shalom that will energize and evoke participation by others who still hold to other ideological loyalties. This changed perception on mission may be illumined by observing two thematic contrasts. First, it is observed by many scholars, especially Jewish scholars, that the theological mind-set and perspective of Genesis is very different from the Moses–Joshua materials that follow. Those latter are conflictual, wreaking of violence, and aimed domination.[11] It is plausible that in the long run, the dominant missional rhetoric of the church is derived from this very old, very conflictual tradition that aims at victory. By contrast, the ancestral narratives in Genesis are largely absent of such conflict and therefore do not aim at triumph or engage in violence. What text we read makes a huge difference about the model of mission we embrace!

A second thematic contrast suggests that *blessing theology* that pervades the ancestral narratives is creation theology. That is, it is concerned for the full functioning of generativity that has been ordained in creation, so that the belated fruitfulness of Israel's mothers is a continuation of the fruitfulness of creation. By contrast, *the redemption traditions* of Moses and Joshua are preoccupied with liberation, emancipation, and transformation, a much more confrontive, disruptive perspective. I understand that one cannot finally separate creation from redemption. But one can make very different accents. I suspect that to avoid the missional triumphalism that has done so much damage and that now feeds the Christian right, an accent on the generosity of creation is a way to refocus mission.

While it is beyond my competence, I suggest that the tension of Genesis/Moses–Joshua, of creation/redemption is a tension that can be seen in the Romans–Galatians axis as it stands a good distance from Colossians and Ephesians. It is well known that the latter think in terms of the mystery of creation. It surely is not

---

11. On the violence endemic in the text, see Schwartz, *The Curse of Cain: The Violent Legacy of Monotheism.*

unimportant that this literature is not a hotbed of doctrinal dispute or of evangelical machismo as Romans and Galatians tend to be.

A Place of Abundance

The two accents on *material-intrinsic* and *bestowal and transference* invite us to think about the church in North America as a place (community) in which God's life-force for a viable future is concentrated. That concentration of God's life-force may be shared with "Gentiles" outside the community who will be blessed. Early on I suggested that the power of curse is characterized by *alienation, anxiety, and brutality.* I am not sure that those are the best words, and I did not linger long over choosing them. The reader may think of better terms by which to characterize the deep distortion that now marks the North American civil community. I have in mind the power of acquisitiveness that reduces everything to a commodity, a pursuit of commodity that is never adequate, that must be pursued by every means available, stopping at nothing to achieve "the most." This disorder has many faces—consumerism, war on the poor, mad militarism, a fascination with technology, child and wife abuse, and championing of prison as social remedy.

Behind all of this deep social alienation, I suspect is the anxiety that there is not enough—not enough for retirement, not enough for education, not enough for medical coverage, not enough for our children, not enough for our community, not enough for our nation, not enough for our church—so we are endlessly under threat. The deeply felt scarcity all around us is a function of an atheism that denies the generosity of the creator and that doubts the abundance of creation. Our North American civic culture is cursed by a sense of scarcity in which the neighbor question evaporates and erstwhile neighbors are seen to be at best inconveniences, more likely as threats.

In the midst of that fearful, feverish pursuit of "enough" sits the church, with its news, its sacraments, its priestly power to bless. The church—the local, organized, visible church—is *a place of abundance*, precisely because in its fidelity the church continues to count on and live from the endless self-giving of God the creator.

Our prayers and our hymns and our texts all attest to the goodness and inexhaustible generosity of God, "who by the power at work within us is able to accomplish abundantly far more than all we can ask or imagine" (Eph 3:20).

This concentration (not monopoly or property) of abundance sits in the midst of the power of curse. It refuses to give in, even though deep among us the seductions of alienation, anxiety, and brutality are at work. It is the primal liturgical task of the church now, I believe, to insist that we will not give in, even though, as always, the power of curse is more compelling and more palpable than is the power of blessing.

Channels of Blessing

This ministry is *by you* . . . blessing.

1. The evangel is *the story* of miraculous abundance. The stories we tell—perhaps even at "children's time"—are about the history of blessing that is put together one episode at a time, that all together tells about abundance that breaks out among us inexplicably. Abraham and Sarah wondered about the power of blessing, and were left in Gen 18:14 with the haunting question: "Is anything too wonderful for Yahweh?" The tradition that bears the evangel asserts that nothing is beyond the creator who blesses. Nothing is impossible! Nothing is too hard! The God who permeates this counter history of blessing is a giver. So Paul taunts his detractors: "What do you have that you did not receive? And if you received it, why do you boast as if it were not a gift?" (1 Cor 4:7). It's all gift!

2. The mission insists on *gestures of charity and generosity*. That is what the church does best . . . modest, visible, intentional acts of neighborliness that entail some giving of self for another. We take that so for granted, and it is often more habitual than it is intentional. But we should at least notice that people caught in cycles of alienation, anxiety, and brutality can give nothing and can notice nothing of abundance. Not to be dismissed are the endless works of canned goods and care packages, of Christmas turkeys and soup kitchens, and of clothing drives and tutoring and shelters—mostly done by nameless saints. All these are overt gestures that refuse to

concede defining authority to the power of curse. Here and there, in face to face contact, concentrated blessing is shared, and people receive power for life.

3. The mission consists in *public actions* that create budgets, policies, and institutions that become channels of blessing. Under the cursed ideology of "privatization," our society just now is in a mood to dismantle everything it can get its hands on. The mandate to Abraham concerning "justice and righteousness," however, makes clear that the power of blessing is not an in-house, church thing to be restricted to acts of charity. Blessing has a public face, for the entire tradition of Israel understands that blessing is a public matter, too urgent to be left intimate. And so the great issues of peace, justice, health, education, housing, and jobs are all facets of blessing "by you."

Abundance in the Midst of Deprivation

It occurs to me that much of the ministry of Jesus is the enactment of abundance in contexts gone sour with deprivation. He is presented in the Gospels as a bodied person who exudes blessing. In Luke 8:44–45, the woman who had tried many failed alternatives came to him: "She came up behind him and touched the fringe of his clothes, and immediately her hemorrhage stopped." Jesus of course noticed: "Who touched me? . . . Someone touched me; for I noticed that power had gone out from me." She is immediately healed, because she had come into contact with his futuring power; she is restored to fullness of life. He does not recruit her or even invite her in. He only blesses her.

In the preceding chapter, John wonders about Jesus' identity (Luke 7:20). Jesus' answer to John is void of explicit theological claim: "The blind receive their sight, the lame walk, the lepers are cleansed, the deaf hear, the dead are raised, the poor have good news brought to them. And blessed is anyone who takes no offense at me" (vv. 22–23). The power to bless exudes from his body and makes all things new. John does not get a neat theological formula; but he now knows everything he needs to know.

We are the people who trail behind Jesus in the history of blessing. What a claim for the church, to be known as the people of limitless resources shared with no restraint, limitless because the abundance of the creator is so trusted that we are persuaded out of our calculating fearfulness![12] The amazing thing is that when "power goes out," it is more than replenished by the creator who continues to bless.

We are fond of saying it is "God's mission," not ours. The purpose is the healing of the Gentiles. The long history is that where there has been that kind of generosity, "loaves abound" . . . as well as members!

12. I am going to end this discussion, because I sense a stewardship sermon coming on!

6

Some Missing Prerequisites

I AM REGULARLY AMAZED by and grateful for the quality of preaching that is being done among us. My impression is that many, many preachers do their work regularly with grace, courage, diligence, and imagination. My comments thus are an attempt to "think with" preachers. My sense is that even among the ablest of preachers, however, the task is very difficult. On the one hand, I sense the enormous, inchoate power of intimidation that operates between preacher and congregation, so that the preacher cannot speak fully and freely the truth she knows, because the congregation will not bear it. To live daily with such silent intimidation from well-intentioned folk is an immobilizing experience. On the other hand, I sense considerable frustration among the more courageous, because when the truthful scandal of the gospel is voiced, it is often wrongly heard or not heard at all. The outcome is that risks of a costly kind have been taken by the preacher to no apparent effect. Such real but ineffective risk, after a while, is debilitating. The constant realities of intimidation and frustration are exceedingly wearing in terms of fatigue, stress, resentment, a sense of defeat, and eventually a failure of nerve.

My assignment here is to think about what is required in order that preaching might be more effective, that is, might evoke serious transformation. My impression is that the issues and problems are largely communal and "systemic," and we have been a long time getting in the condition we are in. Because the issues are communal, systemic, and long in coming, my judgment is that characteristically the preacher is not at fault but is the victim of larger problems, or at best is a coconspirator. The preacher is much more the victim than the perpetrator of ineffectiveness, and I have no intention of "blaming the victim." I suggest three large requirements for effective preaching that for the most part are absent or inoperative in much of our preaching.

An Intentional Embrace of Ecclesiology

Preaching requires *an intentional embrace of an ecclesiology.* That is, effective preaching occurs among those who are prepared to enter into a self-conscious context of speaking and hearing that is committed to and unembarrassed by odd communication. This does not mean that every listener must "believe everything," or that preaching is among the already persuaded; rather this is different communication to which the gathered listeners give some provisional assent. Proclamation takes place in a community of proclamation, and proclamation is its reason for being gathered. When the church gathers for preaching (and for liturgy that is the context of preaching), it gathers with an awareness of having a different identity that permits a different universe of discourse.

1. An intentional ecclesiology makes an assumption about the *cruciality of baptism.* Those who listen to preaching either have accepted baptism or are being invited to baptism. The premise of this odd communication is that we have come prepared to die to what is old in order to be raised to newness of life (Rom 6:4). The gathered listeners either have accepted a distinctive, radically alternative identity and vocation in the world, or are being invited to such a distinctive identity and vocation. In such an environment, different affirmations can be made that do not need to conform to the reason of the world (Rom 12:2). The preacher can make affirmations, utter claims, voice promises, and sound commands that make sense only in a community given to baptism.

A lack of intentional ecclesiology, however, a failure to recognize that this is a baptismal gathering, causes listeners to imagine that there is no peculiar identity or vocation here under consideration. When listening (and therefore speaking) is conducted without baptismal context, very little can be said and less will be heard.

2. An intentional ecclesiology operates with *a distinctive universe of discourse.* We talk differently here and all present are open to that different discourse. Preaching is a conversation that takes place in a certain "language game" to which everyone inchoately subscribes for the extent of the conversation. That universe of discourse is rooted in elemental narrative testimony, going back to the first witnesses who reported their transformation, and is sounded in ways we could describe as prophetic and apostolic. Words, phrases, and speech forms belong to the texture and rationality of this community, and the preacher can operate with freedom in such modes.[1] The preacher does not always need to be looking over her shoulder, justifying her rhetoric according to some other norm or criterion. Where there is lack of consent about our mode of discourse, where there is anxiety about our ways of saying what we are authorized to say, the nerve is cut in communication.

My impression is that the church has been willing to use everyone's language except its own. In conservative contexts, the danger of apostolic narrative has been traded for scholastic language that is reduced to dogmatic assertion and moralism. In liberal contexts, speech among the "cultured despisers" of faith tries to walk carefully around the scandal and ends up a benign affirmation of the status quo. Where the language is uncertain, a great deal of energy is used assuring the listener that nothing will be said that the world regards as foolish or weak. When the preacher moves away from a prophetic, apostolic mode of discourse, there is very little left to say that needs to be said by the preacher.

3. An intentional ecclesiology is deeply linked to the normative character of *the canonical text of Scripture.* The church community has staked its life and its identity on the claims of the scriptural text. The primal witnesses speak. Our faith is given in

---

1. On the cruciality of a specific universe of discourse for transformative communication, see Wolgast, *The Grammar of Justice,* esp. 195–213.

their testimony. This does not mean that there is agreement about the construal or interpretation of the text, but only the expectation that preaching is to see what fresh, live word from God is given and mediated through this text. It follows that the preacher need not be defensive about this text and its use; conversely, the preacher and the congregation are not free to lust after other, "better" texts that are in fact some one else's canonical text, perhaps Freud, or Jung, or Marx, or Parsons, or Geertz, or Whitehead, or Hobbes, or Locke, or whomever.

My impression is that for much of our prattle about "the authority of Scripture," there is very little trust in the truth of the text.[2] On the one hand, critical study has regularly sought something more normative behind the text. On the other hand, what sounds like a "high view of Scripture" is in fact trust in imposed confessional traditions that are rooted, not in the text itself, but in some cultural crisis to which the church has made concrete response. Given the twin temptations of critical suspicion and confessional imposition, we have left little space for the voice of this text itself as the house where God's children may play.[3] We stay embarrassed and tentative about the text, not being aware that it is indeed a counter-text that is not a willing junior partner to any of our other cultural or intellectual commitment. And when the text is not seen as foundational, then the preacher's entire speech begins in jeopardy and without a ground of authority.

My impression is that such an intentional ecclesiology and its elements of baptism, universe of discourse, and text are largely absent in the preaching of our kind of church. At the most, ecclesiology is understood as a form of polity, power, and governance, as in "We are all Presbyterians here." We do not, however, understand this affirmation to refer to our baptism, our modes of discourse, and our canon. Our church identity does not for many people lead to a conclusion:

2. Frei, *The Eclipse of Biblical Narrative*, has traced the power of modernity to cause loss of confidence in narrative; but clearly the issue concerns not simply "narrative," but the authoritative text more generally.

3. The phrase is from Brown, *The Sensus Plenior of Sacred Scripture*, 28.

(a)   that we meet under the aegis of a baptismal identity that endangers all other identities;

(b)   that the purpose of meeting is odd communication that the world describes as foolish; and

(c)   that the text on which we stake our faith is a counter-text and has few epistemological allies in the world.

Where these understandings do not prevail, preaching happens in an intellectual, cultural vacuum in which the preacher scrambles endlessly to make a credible point of contact with the listening congregation that is indifferent to baptism, outside the circle of evangelical discourse, and resistant to normative canon. Where such intentionality is lacking, listening is done through managerial or therapeutic expectations that derive from other cultural contexts that are alien to the scandal.[4] Inevitably, preaching is then miscommunication that almost by definition cannot generate passion for ministry or will for mission.

Social Criticism and Social Possibility

Preaching requires *an explicit practice of social criticism and social possibility discerned in large scope, articulated in close concreteness.* The conversation that is preaching is not in a cultural vacuum and it is not an isolated moment. Consequently, the preacher must have a larger vision of what a sermon intends to do, so that there is long-term strategy about the "human predicament" and the "evangelical possibility" that are juxtaposed in the sermon. Where there is no overarching strategy for the preacher that endures through time from sermon to sermon, no larger sense of crisis, no sustained notion of hope and intentionality, the power of preaching diminishes and descends to triviality and probably mediocrity. When a sermon is not part of a larger sense of our theological situation, the sermon is often reduced to inanity. Sermons then end up as clever ideas, ad

---

4. In making reference to managerial and therapeutic expectations, I am of course alluding to the work of Bellah et al., *Habits of the Heart*.

hoc responses to circumstances of the moment, or the preacher's pet project.

1. The preacher (and it is hoped the congregation) must have some general sense of what the crisis is, in the midst of which they meet. The signs of the crisis are daily and immediate among us: alienated personal relations, distorted power relations, inhumane economic practices. These various pathologies issue in abuse, despair, anxiety, fatigue, and brutality. These several signs, however, are not to be confused with the real issue. We each have, to be sure, our preferred way of identifying the underneath crisis. Some of us believe that the maltreatment of the poor is the focal issue of our time. Some of us imagine that the abuse of the earth and the "greenhouse effect" are most elemental. Some of us have decided that the threat of nuclear arms is the main danger. Some of us conclude that the overriding issue is secularization and the knee jerk response of frightened religion. More personally, we may believe that the issue is distorted sexuality or economics gone awry, so that we cannot afford a house.

All of these judgments witness to the reality of our social context. We need, however, a larger theological articulation. My own inclination is to say that our theological situation consists in the *demise and collapse of the old world of preference and domination* that we have grown to trust and count on. The disappearance of that world, which touches every fact of our life, may indeed be engineered by the rise of the Third World peoples, by the powerful emergence of Islam, or by the release of energy for human liberation. Our theological reality, however, is that God is now dismantling and delegitimating the life-world that most of us have come to know, love, and rely upon. It is the *loss of our known world* that is our common situation. That is our common situation every day, all day, including the days when we gather for preaching and for listening. We are haunted, perhaps troubled, perhaps exhilarated, but haunted. The haunting that pervades our life is daily and concrete.

2. The preacher (and it is hoped the congregation) must have some general sense of the promise and summons of the gospel that is powerfully made to those whose world is ending. All the way from creation to Easter, our canonical text asserts that God is at

work for newness, working something fresh and healing beyond our expectations or data. This general sense is not simply pastoral or therapeutic reassurance, but a *primordial theological conviction that God wills a good future.* As the old world is taken from us, all of us together are summoned to choose, embrace, and receive a new world that is marked by God's outrageous resolve for mercy, justice, compassion, and peace. The move from a world of domination to a world of mercy is a big move, one we make reluctantly, a little at a time.

3. The overarching strategy from sermon to sermon (given these assumptions) requires the practice of social criticism that processes *the ending of a world* to which we cling, and the practice of social possibility that processes *a world emerging* by the power of God, a world we seldom welcome and hesitantly receive. The preaching task, sermon by sermon, text by text, is to enable the listening congregation, one at a time and all together, to relinquish the world dying before our eyes, and to embrace the new world of God's faithfulness that is "at hand," crowding in on us, but only glimpsed most days. Our common situation means that this massive evangelical transformation, wrought through God's ominous discontinuity, is what must be talked about and what may be talked about, in a community grounded in baptism. Moreover, as the congregation meets to hear and to receive, it may be confident that the sermon is the only place in town where an honest conversation is offered about the foundational crisis of our life lived in the presence and in the absence of God. It is not important that the preacher read the crisis exactly as I have characterized it here. It is urgent that the preacher have some "large reading" of public reality, or the chance for serious preaching is forfeited at the outset. The preacher will usefully ask how each particular sermon addresses the ongoing transformative process of our life.

Given such a large sense of crisis, of threat and possibility, the sermon is a mode of communication marked by two important features that are theological in character. First, the sermon is not the time to talk about the deep change that has happened elsewhere, as though the sermon were simply a journalistic report or the minutes of actions taken elsewhere. No, the sermon is the meeting. The sermon is not a report but an event. To the extent that the sermon is indeed the sounding of "the word of God," the very enactment of the sermon enables the listener to make a move from the failed world to the new world God gives. Like a serious therapeutic conversation, the transformation to be accomplished is to be worked here and now in this company, in this speaking and hearing and nowhere else. The sermon is the arena in which people relinquish and receive, and depart changed, renewed, transformed, raised to new life.

Second, this large, almost cosmic drama of transformation is processed a bit at a time, one text at a time, one conversation at a time, through an ongoing parade of images, metaphors, symbols, narratives, memories, and visions. There are two temptations when we use our frail voices on such grand themes. One temptation is to generalize about the crisis; generalization will not do, because we live our lives concretely, one day and one scene at a time. The other temptation is to take a day or a scene in isolation, as though it were not a part of the larger drama. To generalize is to lose the poignancy of the dailyness; to isolate the moment is to miss the larger sense toward which all our moments are gathered.

Effective preaching requires that all our specific, detailed living be understood as a part of a larger drama being acted out in the presence of God. Effective preaching requires that all our specific, detailed texts be understood as crafted exposes of the story of our life with God. Our lives are about only a few things; those, however, are of utmost seriousness. Our scatteredness, however, tempts us to imagine that there is no larger drift or sense either to our life, or to God's word toward us.

Where the sense of largeness is lacking, where we do not understand the crisis of great loss or the alternative of great newness, sermons are twittered away in good advice, happy reassurances, or harsh intimidation. The outcome of such twittering is the desperate sense that my life really is not about anything. Then nothing is expected and nothing can be counted on. The power of technical reason that apportions reality into operational units robs us of any wholeness that permits mission. Where there is no larger sense in preaching, we likely will not understand our crisis nor discern God's alternative for us.

Self-critical Hermeneutics

Preaching requires an *intentional self-critical hermeneutic about authority, transformation, and communication.* Put more simply, there is need for a thoughtful awareness of who speaks, who listens, and what happens. I have no doubt that much of an effective hermeneutic happens accidentally. My impression is that we could be much more intentional and explicit about the dramatic dimensions of the preaching enterprise.

1. *Who speaks.* Of course it is the preacher who speaks; we are all schooled in the conviction that preaching is "truth mediated through personality." No doubt. That correct affirmation, however, is freighted with problems that evoke intimidation and frustration. Not without cause have we insisted that preaching is proclamation of God's word and that the text proclaimed contains God's word.[5] Such claims are endlessly problematic and at times exploited in arrogant and authoritarian ways, as though the preacher could speak *ex cathedra.*

A hermeneutic of God's word, however, means something other than license for the preacher. It means that the congregation gathers to be addressed by God's speech, by the sounding of God's purpose, will, character, and promise. At its best, preaching is indeed a voice other than our own. The authority of such speech is other than the claim of the preacher; that which is said is (and had better be) a disclosure other than the opinion of the preacher. This is indeed the holy moment of address when none other than God "calls into existence things that do not exist" (Rom 4:17). The speech of this God is always "yes" (2 Cor 1:19–20), though God's life-giving "yes" contradicts our treasured idolatries. The speech of God is specific, concrete, and crafted. God's summoning, forming work is done as does the artist; God forms what did not exist before

---

5. The daring claim that proclamation is indeed "God's word" has been exposited in a magisterial way by Barth, *Church Dogmatics* I/1: *The Doctrine of the Word of God*, 98–111.

the moment of artistry. The moment of such crafting and forming is not for "projects," but for the giving of God's majestic self.

2. *Who listens.* The ones gathered are either the baptized or the ones summoned to baptism. Our lives, however, are endlessly complicated so that a baptized ear has to sort out the static. I suggest that this odd communication concerns those who are on overload, who resist authority, and who are nearly talked out of a capacity to respond. We do not easily listen in our society and we do not want to be addressed.[6]

We are on overload because we live in the midst of din and hammering appeals, all seeking a piece of our commitment. After a while, we can hardly sort out the voices; we grow indifferent, not wanting to hear any of them. We are exhausted by much speaking that contains no serious speech, that surely never offers an unqualified "yes."

We are resistant to authority. The ideology of modernity nurtures us to refuse access to anyone concerning the serious places in our life. We are deluded enough by "democratic" myths and notions of self-sufficiency, that we are prone to listen only to voices that echo our vested interest.[7] As a result, we are not much inclined to the authority of the preacher. Beyond that, we are not much inclined to be addressed by a "voice of holiness" that makes a total claim and that subverts the underpinning of our carefully arranged lives. We will listen only to lesser voices of lesser claims that are comfortably domesticated. The problem of course is that lesser voices make only innocuous gifts and promises too easily credible.

3. *What happens.* There meet in preaching the holy "yes" of God and the befogged ears of the almost baptized. In that moment of speech, we anticipate the breaking of conformity and the working

6. See Ellul, *The Humiliation of the Word*; and more popularly, Postman, *Amusing Ourselves to Death.*

7. On the cruciality of listening for living, see Rosenstock-Huessy, *Speech and Reality.* In paraphrasing and challenging Descartes, Rosenstock-Huessy writes: "The first outcry of human self-consciousness about society is the word 'Listen.' And as long as this word is not recognized as the cornerstone of our whole building of social science, this science will never come of age. *Audi, ut vivamus.* 'Listen and we shall survive.' *Audi, ne monamur.* 'Listen, lest we die.' Human survival and revival depend on speech" (23–25).

of transformation (Rom 12:2). The aim of evangelical preaching is indeed transformation. What is lacking among us is attention to the ways in which transformation happens and the kinds of wondrous, miraculous speech that permits, authorizes, and energizes such change. We preachers might well ask of our own experience: Who changed us? How do we change? Who said what that gave us newness?

I am persuaded that transformative speech is never didactic, never systemic, never moralistic, because such speech either reinforces what we already thought (and so occasions no change), or it drives us to defensiveness (which never evokes change). Speech that transforms us is speech that breaks the grip of present tense reality, that envisions and imagines an alternative world, that moves us outside our guarded preconceptions and our treasured non-negotiables.[8] Such speech is characteristically poetic, playful, dramatic, and artistic—dangerously open-ended, not offering conventional certitudes, but affirming possibilities not grounded in our present controlled arrangements. This means that the speech evoking transformation is unlike almost all other speech in our society. It is unlike other speech in *what is said,* for it has as its subject the Holy One who is never a predictable character to plot. It is unlike other speech in *how it is said,* for the *how* of imagination is linked to the *what* of gospel.[9]

Preaching that is done in the context of U.S. culture now occurs in an odd circumstance. On the one hand, the old power arrangements and the trusted epistemological certitudes have failed, and are at least in jeopardy.[10] We have much less to count on than

8. On the cruciality of speech for liberation and subversion, see Green, *Imaging God.*

9. On the cruciality of "how" for "what," see O'Day, *The Word Disclosed,* 11–15 and passim; and Coles, *Times of Surrender,* 45–46, with reference to William Carlos Williams: "'It's important,' he once said, 'to listen not only to the complaints of your patients but how they put them into words for you— how they choose to say (and regard) what they want to tell you.'"

10. On the epistemological subversiveness of the gospel, see Welch, *Communities of Resistance and Solidarity.* For a more theoretical reflection on the epistemological crisis, see Horkheimer, "The End of Reason." On the epistemological crisis, Horkheimer writes: "Pain is the means of calling men back

we used to. On the other hand, the old "Christian consensus" no longer compels wide public assent. Indeed, there seems to be assent mostly where our interests are reiterated as "truth." As a result, preaching no longer happens (except in rare, very protected places) from an assured, accepted center. More likely, Christian proclamation is a voice at the margin, or at the most a voice in the cacophony that is granted no cultural priority or privilege. Old expectations of authority simply do not operate.

That difficult moment of preaching in our culture is also a moment of enormous possibility for new courage and freedom in preaching. Because the difficulty is also a possibility, it is important that we be *intentional about a communal identity* rooted in a text and embraced in baptism. It is crucial that we be *thoughtful and honest about the large social reality* that places us commonly in a crisis. It is urgent that we *think through our speech situation* that may let us speak and hear differently, trustingly, and obediently. The notions of *ecclesiology, social criticism, and hermeneutics* may sound too abstract. I mean only to think again about the powerful, but largely unacknowledged accomplishments of modernity that have robbed preaching of its conventional percentages. It is my expectation that intentionality about these three items will permit a new authority—not like that of the scribes (Mark 1:22!)—an authority that gives life. The preacher, like the word, may be freshly unfettered. Someday soon preachers may stand in the pulpit and notice that the immobilizing powers of modernity have been broken. It will be a day! It will be some sermon! It will be some miracle, the miracle to which we draw nearer each time we preach faithfully.

---

from the noumenal world into which all empiricist philosophers and even Kant forbade them to penetrate. It was always the best teacher to bring men to reason. Pain leads the resistant and wayward, the phantast and Utopian back to themselves. It reduces them to the body, to part of the body. Pain levels and equalizes everything, man and man, man and animal," 46.

7

Walk Humbly with Your God

THE FAMOUS TRIAD OF Mic 6:8 comes as the culmination of a long disputatious transaction between Yahweh and Israel that is performed by the prophet.

How Shall We Come before Yahweh?

In Mic 6:1–2 there is a summons to court in which Yahweh enters into a juridical dispute ("controversy") with Israel. Yahweh states Yahweh's case against Israel (vv. 3–5): Yahweh has been generously faithful, and Israel has been perfidious "from Shittim to Gilgal." The question of v. 6 explores Israel's appropriate response to the case Yahweh has made. What is now asked of Israel after the contrast of divine generosity and human treachery? It is odd and noteworthy that the question is asked of "man" (Adam). In a parallel posing of the same question in Deut 10:12, the question is addressed to Israel. The double address of Mic 6:8 and Deut 10:12 suggests that the question posed to Israel is, *mutatis mutandis*, the same question the creator puts to Adam, that is, to all humanity. The primal question for Israel and for humanity is how to come before Yahweh when the relationship has been fractured.

Prior to v. 8, the same question is asked in v. 6 in a slightly different form. The proposed answer in vv. 6–7 is a "false answer":

burnt offerings, calves, a thousand of rams, ten thousand rivers of oil, my first born. It is commonly noticed that the answer builds from the least valuable to the most valuable. But every part of the answer is a commodity. The answer ponders how one offers something "of value." The re-asking of the question in v. 8 indicates, without explanatory comment, that the "commodity answer" is wrong and rejected. Yahweh does not want "stuff" from Israel or from humanity (see Ps 50:8–13).

It is only after the false proposal of vv. 6–7 that the question is again posed in v. 8. The question implies and assumes a certain positioning between Yahweh and Israel or between Yahweh and humanity. Yahweh asks and Israel must respond. Yahweh "requires" and humanity must answer. The God of generous rescue (v. 4) is the God who must be obeyed. The Lord of the exodus is the commander of Sinai. Or in Barthian language, the God of the gift (*Gabe*) is the one who assigns a task (*Aufgabe*).

Faithful Relationships and Reliable Solidarity

Being warned in vv. 6–7 that the right response to the requirements of Yahweh is not material commodity, v. 8 now answers appropriately that the God of the covenant wants faithful relationships and reliable solidarity. The famous triad, upon close encounter, makes clear that the first two "commands" bespeak Israel's most familiar vocabulary of covenantal solidarity:

— To "do justice" (*mishpat*) is to be sure that the neighbor is well provided for;

— To "love kindness" (*chesed*) is to practice a life of reliable solidarity. ("Kindness" is a notoriously weak translation of the term.)

The two terms, *mishpat* and *chesed*, stand at the center of Israel's faith-talk. Indeed *mishpat* most often comes in a pair with *tsedeqah* (righteousness), and *chesed* most often comes in a pair with 'amunah ("faithfulness"). If we extrapolate according to Israel's preferred rhetorical practice, we are given Israel's two most important word pairs—"justice and righteousness" and "steadfast love and faithfulness"—that echo with love of neighbor and love of God. The first pair, "justice and righteousness," concerns the neighborhood. The second pair, "steadfast love and faithfulness," concerns love of God, so that Micah's first two components allude to "the two great commandments."

Alas, in the third component, the one assigned to me, there is no such defining vocabulary from Israel's tradition. The phrase "walk humbly with your God" does not give much to work with and evokes no spectacular connections. We get five words that invite an Israelite (human) response to Yahweh that is perhaps even beyond the first two commandments of love of neighbor and love of God.

Walking the Path

The command concerns "humble walking." "Walking" in the Bible is a metaphor for a life journey or a life performance. "Being on the way" is a life chance and a life performance. It refers to Torah-obedience and is transposed in the New Testament into discipleship as Christians are "followers of the way," the way of Torah, the way of Jesus, the way of well-being. Thus in Deuteronomic theology (on which see Ps 1:1), Solomon is to "walk in the ways" (1 Kgs 3:14; see 8:23, 25), but Manasseh, the model of disobedience, walked in the way of idols (2 Kgs 21:22). That entire theology concerns a choice between "two paths," one that is wide and leads to death, one that is narrow and yields life (Deut 30:15–20; Matt 7:13–14). Decisions are always being made about the paths and their different outcomes. In our Micah passage, Israel is summoned to a path of "justice" and "kindness." That opens two questions: *How* to walk? *With whom* to walk?

How Shall We Walk?

The question of *how to walk* is answered here: "Humbly." The term is misleading in translation, however, because it may suggest groveling self-abasement that is much embraced in much fraudulent piety. Nothing, of course, could be further from the intent of this prophetic poetry. Israel is never summoned to groveling self-abasement, and the church has a great deal to unlearn about that, notably concerning Lenten disciplines.

Surprisingly the term "humble" occurs only one other time in the Old Testament, and therefore that other usage is important for our study:

> When pride comes, then comes disgrace;
> but wisdom is to the humble. (Prov 11:2)

As is usual in such two-line proverbs, there is a contrast between the two lines (two paths), each of which comes with inescapable and predictable futures. The positive claim is: Humbleness will yield wisdom. This is a primary conviction of the book of Proverbs. We are helped in understanding "humble" by the parallel line that state the antithesis: Pride will yield disgrace (shame). Appealing to the double use of the word "comes," Christine Yoder suggests that pride and disgrace are "traveling companions."[1] They arrive together. When pride arrives, shame will arrive along with it. The learner may expect to have either *shame* or *wisdom*, and the choice will come by the behavioral option of "humble" or "prideful." Thus "to walk humbly" is the opposite of walking proudly, that is strutting. On strutting, see Prov 30:28–31, where the wisdom teachers mockingly identify four "strutters": a lion, a rooster, a he-goat, a king—all macho images of self-exhibition and self-importance.[2] As we have seen recently with so many "self-righteous" politicians and ministers, such a *strutting* way often leads to *embarrassment*, and the wisdom teachers could see such embarrassment coming a long way off. Such prideful strutting bespeaks arrogance, self-sufficiency, autonomy, the need to occupy center stage, the sense that I am the only one on the set.

In reading up for this exposition, I have been instructed by two studies, both of which have suggested that "'walking humbly,'" in contrast to strutting, is to pay attention to *the other*, or in more elitist talk, "alterity," that is, to recognize that on the path with me

1. Yoder, *Proverbs*, 131.

2. Ibid., 286. Yoder, more generously, refers to these four as "magisterial, fearless."

are others from whom one receives one's identity. "Walking humbly" means to be on the path with them, to be in relation to them and with reference to them on the way. The strutter acknowledges no other, and imagines he needs no other and may end in despair. Thus the phrasing of Micah answers the question of "how to walk" by calling attention to the need and inescapability of the others who walk with us on the path of life. Indeed God requires that we walk with the other. Bruce Ellis Benson writes:

> The Christian can only offer them [the teachings of Christ] in a spirit of deep humility, precisely because they are examples of being truly humble, of being dependent on one another, of loving even those who do not love us back. Of course, even these examples must be offered up in political discourse only in a spirit of respect and with a willingness to dialogue with the other . . . rather than starting by focusing on *me*, the focus begins on the other. Of course this is fully in line with what Jesus says. His injunctions are what one does *in response to the other*—whether the widow, the stranger, the enemy, or the one who demands one's clothing. In regard to these last two, Jesus in effect says, "Do the opposite of what you would be inclined to do"—instead of hating in return, love; instead of resisting the demand, give freely of even that which is not demanded. In not responding in kind, one changes the entire structure of the relation: it is now structured by love.[3]

Lisa Fullam, in her exposition of Thomistic thought, champions "other-centered solidarity" and "paying attention" as ingredients in a life of authentic humility.[4]

With Whom Shall We Walk?

We may now ask our second question: If we walk the path humbly, acknowledging "the other," who will be our companion along the way? The answer to this question is given by Micah, "with your

3. Benson, "Radical Democracy and Radical Christianity," 253.

4. Fullam, *The Virtue of Humility*, 120, 184–85.

God." There are many uses of phrases like "walk in the way of God," and in Mic 4:5 it is to "walk in the name of God." But here it is "with God." I do not know if there are other uses of this formulation. Whether unique or at least rare, the imagery is that of direct and immediate companionship with God, so that one's way of life is with reference to and in the company of, this God who willingly walks with us on the path. The strutter has no companion, surely not the God of Exodus–Sinai, the Lord of Friday–Sunday.

The phrasing is terse. It is only "your God." We can, of course, unpack the phrase in rich and thick ways. First of all the companion God of the walk is, according to the first two elements in Micah's statement, the God of justice and kindness. These core words of faith refer first of all to the qualities experienced in Israel's life with Yahweh. It is Yahweh who wills and practices restorative justice. It is Yahweh who embodies and exhibits steadfastness. It is Yahweh whose very presence on the path redefines the path of life according to neighborly justice and covenantal solidarity. This companion is not just a good feeling or a happy intimacy, but carries along on the way an entire re-characterization of reality as a relational enterprise that both reassures and summons.

Beyond the two words in our verse, justice and kindness, the companion God is the God of the entire saving tradition, so that one walks with the God who saves and feeds and reconciles and heals and forgives and transforms. Thus, for example, Moses, pondering the next leg of the journey to the land of promise, can say to Yahweh with some tone of insistence: "If your presence will not go, do not carry us up from here" (Exod 33:15). Moses requires Yahweh's companionship; and Yahweh agrees to travel with Moses and with Israel on the way . . . when Israel walks "humbly" with God.

Now we have Micah's two defining qualifications for the walk:

—*How:* Humbly . . . with reference to the other;

—*Who:* with Yahweh, the companion God of transformative well-being.

Traveling with the Incommensurate One

It remains for the preacher to transpose this redefined *travel with companionship* into a contemporary possibility. One may begin with the commitment of our consumer society to strutting autonomy. This is evident in the excessive virility of athletes who must not only win, but must make gestures of triumph in the dismantling of the opponent. And even in suburban families, every little achievement by a young child . . . a refrigerator door drawing, "graduating" from first grade, arriving in church after Sunday School . . . must be treated in such a society as an awesome accomplishment. The assumption is that esteem and enhancement will generate more adequate personhood. It seems clear, in more careful perspective, that such celebration that evokes strutting . . . upon which the consumer society depends . . . produces endless need for satiation and eventually narcissicism.

The covenantal tradition of the gospel offers an alternative form of life that does not depend upon self-enhancement and congratulations. It depends rather on self-abandoning companionship along the way, for it is the act of companionship (and not self-celebration) that gives staying power, self-respecting dignity, and eventually well-being. The contrast between *self-announcing strutting* and *self-giving alterity* is a defining stress point in our society, a point at which the church offers a genuine alternative. It is an alternative that is pervasive in sapiential perspective, one that is rooted in the God of the gospel who does not need to strut. Indeed, Paul's Christological hymn is to the point (Phil 2:5–11):

—Jesus could have strutted: he was in the form of God.

—Instead he gave himself for the ones on the path of obedience: he emptied himself and became obedient.

—He arrived at great affirmation from God who stands with such self-giving; therefore God has highly exalted him.

Thus the great triad of Micah reflects the path of life—required by God of Israel and of Adam—in terms of *the other* on the path with us who precludes our traveling alone in arrogance or in despair. On the one hand, we notice, as Israel always noticed, that the companion God of covenant is totally incommensurate with us. This God may travel with us, but this God is radically unlike us, and we may not imagine that this traveling companion is only "a good buddy." This traveling companion who willingly walks with us is creator of heaven and earth, but who on the path has no need to call attention to such asymmetry. It is like being helped by a "famous" person who does not need to call attention to self. This incommensurate quality of the other as companion is well attested by Alan Paton in his poem addressed to his young son:

> Do not pronounce judgment on the Infinite, nor suppose God to be like a bad Prime Minister.
> Do not suppose him powerless, or if powerful, malignant.
> Do not address your mind to criticisms of the Creator, do not pretend to know his categories.
> Do not take his universe in your hand, and point out its defects with condescension.
> Do not think he is a greater potentate, a manner of President of the United Galaxies.
> Do not think that because you know so few human beings, that he is in a comparable though more favorable position.
> Do not think it absurd that he should know every sparrow, or number the hairs of your head.
> Do not compare him with yourself, nor suppose your human love to be an example to shame him.
> He is not greater than Plato or Lincoln nor superior to Shakespeare and Beethoven.
> He is their God, their powers and their gifts proceeded from Him.
> In infinite darkness they poured with their fingers over the first word of the Book of his Knowledge.[5]

This is the breath-taking truth of "walking humbly with your God"! This is God! And we travel along!

But on the other hand, if we look closely at the one who travels with us in hiddenness and without calling attention, we notice an

5. Paton, "Meditation for a Young Boy Confirmed."

odd thing. *The other* to be noticed in our genuine alterity is not a holy God, "immortal, invisible, only wise." Rather the one on the path with us takes the form of sister and brother; of widow and orphan; of publican and sinner; of lame, leper, dead, needy, who in their neediness are ready to travel and have gifts to give. We are mindful of the vexing linkage Jesus made about traveling with the least:

> Truly I tell you, just as you did it to one of *the least* of these who are members of my family, you did it to me . . . Truly I tell you, just as you did not do it to one of *the least* of these, you did not do it to me. (Matt 25:40, 45)

Along the path we blink and do a double take, like a "rabbit and a duck." Our companion is *the incommensurate other* who is *the least*, or conversely, *the least* whom we encounter is *the incommensurate one* from whom we receive life. Either way, "we never walk alone" when we perform justice and kindness. The alternative to this traveling mercy is one to which we are frequently seduced. That alternative path that is wide leaves us all alone when in fact we are made for companionship. We are made for companionship by the God who is willing to be seen with us, in public, on the way. No groveling, no self-abasement. Such companionship yields a joyous satisfaction that our strutting can never produce.

Bibliography

Anderson, Bernhard W. *Creation versus Chaos: Reinterpretation of Mythical Symbolism in the Bible.* 1967. Reprinted, Eugene, OR: Wipf & Stock, 2005.

———. *The Unfolding Drama of the Bible.* 4th ed. Minneapolis: Fortress, 2006.

Barth, Karl. *Church Dogmatics* I/1: *The Doctrine of the Word of God.* Translated by G. T. Thomson. New York: Scribners, 1936.

Bellah, Robert et al. *Habits of the Heart: Individualism and Commitment in American Life.* Berkeley: University of California Press, 1985.

Benson, Bruce Ellis. "Radical Democracy and Radical Christianity." *Political Theology* 10 (2009) 247–59

Berquist, Jon L. *Judaism in Persia's Shadow: A Social and Historical Approach.* 1995. Reprinted, Eugene, OR: Wipf & Stock, 2003.

Berry, Wendell. *Standing by Words: Essays.* San Francisco: North Point Press, 1983.

Brown, Raymond E. *The Sensus Plenior of Sacred Scripture.* 1955. Reprinted, Eugene, OR: Wipf & Stock, 2008.

Brueggemann, Walter. *Biblical Perspectives on Evangelism: Living in a Three-Storied Universe.* Nashville: Abingdon, 1993.

———. *Cadences of Home: Preaching among Exiles.* Louisville: Westminster John Knox, 1997.

———. "Ecumenism as the Shared Practice of a Peculiar Identity." *Word & World* 18 (1998) 122–35.

———. "Faith with a Price." *The Other Side* 34/4 (1998) 32–35.

———. "The Kerygma of the Priestly Writers." *Zeitschrift für die alttestamentliche Wissenschaft* 84 (1972) 397–413. Reprinted in Walter Brueggemann and Hans Walter Wolff, *The Vitality of Old Testament Traditions,* 101–13. 2nd ed. Atlanta: John Knox, 1982.

———. *The Land: Place as Gift, Promise, and Challenge in Biblical Faith.* 2nd ed. Minneapolis: Fortress, 2002.

———. *The Prophetic Imagination.* 2nd ed. Minneapolis: Fortress, 2001.

———. *Theology of the Old Testament: Testimony, Dispute, Advocacy.* Minneapolis: Fortress Press, 1997.

Buber, Martin. *The Kingship of God.* London: Allen & Unwin, 1967.

Bibliography

Coles, Robert. *Times of Surrender: Selected Essays*. Iowa City: University of Iowa Press, 1988.

Coulson, John. *Religion and Imagination: "In Aid of a Grammar of Assent."* Oxford: Clarendon, 1981.

Craddock, Fred B. *Overhearing the Gospel*. Lyman Beecher Lecture 1978. Nashville: Abingdon, 1978.

Donahue, John R. *The Gospel in Parable: Metaphor, Narrative, and Theology in the Synoptic Gospels*. Philadelphia: Fortress, 1988.

Ellul, Jacques. *The Humiliation of the Word*. Translated by Joyce Main Hanks. Grand Rapids: Eerdmans, 1985.

———. *The Technological Society*. Translated by John Wilkinson. New York: Random House, 1967.

Frei, Hans. *The Eclipse of the Biblical Narrative*. New Haven: Yale University Press, 1974.

Fretheim, Terence E. *Deuteronomic History*. Interpreting Biblical Texts. Nashville: Abingdon, 1983.

Fullam, Lisa. *The Virtue of Humility: A Thomistic Apologetic*. Hors Series. Lewiston, NY: Mellen, 2009.

Green, Garrett. *Imaging God: Theology and the Religious Imagination*. San Francisco: Harper & Row, 1989.

Hall, Douglas John. *Waiting for Gospel: An Appeal to the Dispirited Remnants of Protestant "Establishment."* Eugene, OR: Cascade Books, 2012.

———. *What Christianity Is Not: An Exercise in "Negative" Theology*. Eugene, OR: Cascade Books, 2013.

Hamilton, Jeffries M. *Social Justice and Deuteronomy: The Case of Deuteronomy 15*. SBL Dissertation Series 136. Atlanta: Scholars, 1992.

Hanson, K. C. "'How Honorable! How Shameful!' A Cultural Analysis of Matthew's Makarisms and Reproaches." *Semeia* 68 (1994[96]) 81–111.

Herzog, William R., II. *Parables as Subversive Speech: Jesus as Pedagogue of the Oppressed*. Louisville: Westminster John Knox, 1994.

Horkheimer, Max. "The End of Reason." In *The Essential Frankfurt School Reader*, edited by Andrew Arato and Eike Gebhardt, 26–48. New York: Continuum, 1982.

Hunsberger, George R. *Bearing the Witness of the Spirit: Lesslie Newbigin's Theology of Cultural Pluralism*. Grand Rapids: Eerdmans, 1998.

Kierkegaard, Soren[set slash through o]. *Either/Or I*. 2 vols. Translated by Howard V. Hong and Edna H. Hong. Kierkegaard's Writings 3–4. Princeton: Princeton University Press, 1987.

Klein, Ralph W. *Israel in Exile*. Overtures to Biblical Theology. Philadelphia: Fortress, 1980.

Koch, Klaus. "Is There a Doctrine of Retribution in the Old Testament?" In *Theodicy in the Old Testament*, edited by James L. Crenshaw, 57–87. Issues in Religion and Theology. Philadelphia: Fortress, 1983.

Levenson, Jon D. *The Death and Resurrection of the Beloved Son: The Transformation of Child Sacrifice in Judaism and Christianity.* New Haven: Yale University Press, 1993.

———. *Resurrection and the Restoration of Israel: The Ultimate Victory of the God of Life.* New Haven: Yale University Press, 2006.

Neusner, Jacob. *The Enchantments of Judaism: Rites of Transformation from Birth through Death.* New York: Basic Books, 1987.

O'Day, Gail R. *The Word Disclosed: John's Story and Narrative Preaching.* St. Louis: CBP, 1987.

Paton, Alan. "Meditation for a Young Boy Confirmed." *Christian Century,* October 13, 1954, 1238. Reprinted in *Knocking on the Door,* 89–90. London: SPCK, 1959.

Postman, Neil. *Amusing Ourselves to Death: Public Discourse in the Age of Show Business.* New York: Penguin, 1986.

Rad, Gerhard von. "The Form-critical Problem of the Hexateuch." In *The Problem of the Hexateuch and Other Essays,* 1–78. Translated by E. W. Trueman Dicken. New York: McGraw-Hill, 1966.

———. *Old Testament Theology.* Vol. 1, *The Theology of the Historical Traditions.* Translated by D. M. G. Stalker. 1962. Reprinted with a Foreword by Walter Brueggemann. Old Testament Library. Louisville: Westminster John Knox, 2001.

———. *Wisdom in Israel.* Translated by James D. Martin. Nashville: Abingdon, 1972.

Ricoeur, Paul. *Figuring the Sacred: Religion, Narrative, and Imagination.* Edited by Mark I. Wallace. Minneapolis: Fortress, 1995.

Rosenstock-Huessy, Eugen. *Speech and Reality.* Norwich, VT: Argo, 1970.

Schwartz, Regina M. *The Curse of Cain: The Violent Legacy of Monotheism.* Chicago: University of Chicago Press, 1997.

Scott, Bernard Brandon. *Hear Then the Parable: A Commentary on the Parables of Jesus.* Minneapolis: Fortress, 1989.

Walzer, Michael. *Interpretation and Social Criticism.* The Tanner Lectures on Human Values. Cambridge: Harvard University Press, 1987.

Welch, Sharon D. *Communities of Resistance and Solidarity: A Feminist Theology of Liberation.* Maryknoll, NY: Orbis, 1985.

Westermann, Claus. *Blessing in the Bible and the Life of the Church.* Translated by Keith R. Crim. Overtures to Biblical Theology. Philadelphia: Fortress, 1978.

———. *Creation.* Translated by John J. Scullion. Philadelphia: Fortress, 1974.

———. "Creation and History in the Old Testament." In *The Gospel and Human Destiny,* edited by Vilmos Vajta, 11–38. Minneapolis: Augsburg, 1971.

———. "Sprache und Struktur der Prophetie Deuterojesajas." In *Neudrucke und Berichte aus dem 20 Jahrhundert,* 92–170. Theologische Bücherei 24. Munich: Kaiser, 1964.

———. *What Does the Old Testament Say about God?* Sprunt Lectures. Atlanta: John Knox, 1979.

Bibliography

White, James Boyd. *Living Speech: Resisting the Empire of Force*. Princeton: Princeton University Press, 2006.

Wilder, Amos. "Story and Story-World." *Interpretation* 37 (1983) 353–64.

Wilson, Woodrow. "How Books Become Immortal." *The Atlantic Monthly* (Jan/ Feb 2006) 58–60.

Witte, John, Jr. *God's Joust, God's Justice: Law and Religion in the Western Tradition*. Grand Rapids: Eerdmans, 2006.

Wolgast, Elizabeth H. *The Grammar of Justice*. Ithaca, NY: Cornell University Press, 1987.

Wolff, Hans Walter. "The Kerygma of the Yahwist." *Interpretation* 20 (1966) 131–58. Reprinted in Walter Brueggemann and Hans Walter Wolff, *The Vitality of Old Testament Traditions*, 41–66. 2nd ed. Atlanta: John Knox, 1982.

Yoder, Christine Roy. *Proverbs*. Abingdon Old Testament Commentaries. Nashville: Abingdon, 2009.

Index of Scripture

Index of Names

www.ingramcontent.com/pod-product-compliance
Lightning Source LLC
Chambersburg PA
CBHW020208090426
42734CB00008B/979